Tropical Marine Aquaria

Graham F. Cox

Illustrated by George Thompson

HAMLYN

FOREWORD

In this book an attempt has been made to give a basic appreciation of the principles involved in the successful home-culture of tropical marine life-forms.

Full details are given of how to establish each of the three currently popular biosystems for the culture of marine life. For ease of reference these have been christened the natural, semi-natural and clinical methods. Almost all of the commonly imported coral fishes and invertebrates from the Red Sea, Caribbean, East Africa and the Philippines are illustrated and their basic requirements are dealt with in detail.

Since this relatively small book covers every aspect of marine aquarium technology, it has been necessary to impose a limitation on the amount of text, particularly in the more detailed technical sections. Nevertheless, all the basic principles and equipment are discussed and it is hoped that the book will be of value as a complete introductory guide to the hobby.

The author would like to express his sincere thanks to George Thompson, the illustrator of this book, for his unrelenting determination faithfully to duplicate both the colours and form of the marine animals. Infinite pains were taken and the vast majority of the paintings are from life thus avoiding the chromatic aberration so frequently found in colour photographs.

G.F.C.

Published by Hamlyn Publishing
Bridge House, London Road, Twickenham, Middlesex

First published in paperback 1971
Hardback edition published 1985

ISBN 0 600 30651 8

Printed in Italy

CONTENTS

INTRODUCTION

Considering the apparently exorbitant prices of tropical marine animals (fishes and invertebrates), it is not surprising that complete newcomers to this absorbing new hobby, and even experienced freshwater aquarists, sometimes query the advantages of setting up a tropical marine aquarium.

Some of the most fascinating creatures on this planet are invertebrates, and the largest and most imposing of these are found in salt water, and not in bodies of fresh water. There are, of course, some invertebrate life-forms found in fresh water and some of these, such as *Daphnia*, snails and *Tubifex* worms, various aquatic insects and their larvae, do occur in freshwater aquaria, although usually they are present as undesirable pests or as deliberately introduced live food. However, when you own a sea aquarium your horizons are limited only by the size of your tank. In your home you can witness the majestic power of a large cowrie as it 'lawnmowers' its way around the algae in your tank; the unforgettable beauty of a pink and white nudibranch mollusc as, with ballerina-like grace, it undulates through the water; the sinewy power of an octopus as it insidiously flows towards its unsuspecting prey; or the flowery form of the gently waving tentacles of a predatory anemone.

For those people who prefer their pleasures to proceed at a fast and furious pace, the relative calm of the solely invertebrate aquarium may not have much appeal. The non-stop activity and unbelievable colours of the coral-reef fishes must be enough to satisfy even this preference however, whilst for those who like the best of both worlds, it is quite possible to combine both invertebrates and fishes in the same marine aquarium.

Finally, many of the more startling discoveries recently made concerning the nature and habits of coral-reef organisms, have come about as a result of the work of non-professional biologists carefully studying the inhabitants of their home sea aquaria. For example, what were once thought to be three distinctly different species of fishes within the wrasse family were discovered to be merely maturation colour changes of the same species Clown Wrasse (*Coris gaimard*).

Maturation colour changes in the Clown Wrasse

DIFFERENCES BETWEEN CORAL FISHES AND FRESHWATER FISHES

An important difference between the body chemistry of seawater fishes and their freshwater relatives is caused simply by the difference of salt concentration, and hence density, between sea water and fresh water. The 'strength' of the solutions making up the tissue fluids of a seawater fish is lower than that of surrounding water in which the animal lives, i.e., it is less dense. As a result of the natural phenomenon known as *osmosis*, when a semi-permeable membrane (such as the surface tissues of a fish) separates a low-concentration solution from a high-concentration solution, there is a tendency for water molecules to move through that membrane from the former solution to the latter. This is exactly the situation in a fish living in sea water. To counteract the continual loss of water to its environmental fluid, the seawater fish has a relatively high freshwater requirement. It undoubtedly obtains some of its pure water supplies from food, either directly or by chemically breaking down complex substances, but these supplies are not sufficient in themselves and the

By osmosis, the marine fish continually loses water to its environment. To compensate for this, pure water is obtained from sea water drunk in large quantities.

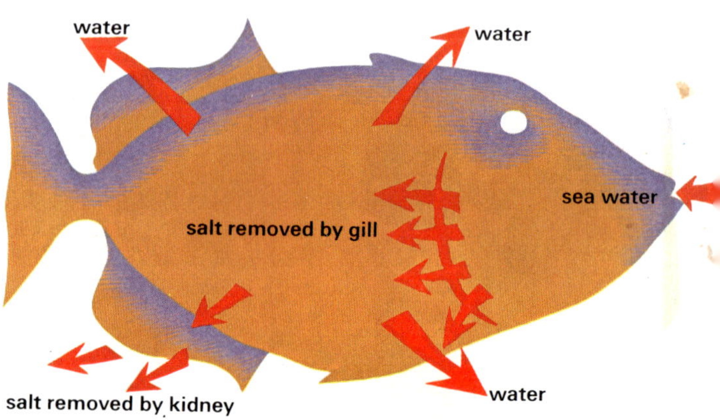

seawater fish continually drinks in sea water. It must then extract the various salts from solution and those which it does not need (which are in the vast majority) are excreted through salt-secreting cells in the gills and also as waste from the kidney.

If the reader has followed the rather complex explanations above, he will immediately realize that because the body fluids of the freshwater fish are *hypertonic* (stronger or more concentrated) in relation to its environmental fluid, the animal faces the problems of the seawater fish in reverse. By osmosis the freshwater fish is continually taking up water through the surface tissues and is in danger of 'flooding' or 'drowning', and must therefore continually secrete water at a high rate.

One is always amazed at the metabolic versatility of the *euryhaline* fishes such as the Salmon (*Salmo salar*), the Malayan Angel (*Monodactylus argenteus*), and the Scat (*Scatophagus argus*), which are quite capable of adapting their body chemistry processes to either a marine or freshwater existence. Unfortunately, however, most of our coral fishes are *stenohaline*, in that they are unable to move freely from sea water to fresh water and back again.

Conversely, the freshwater fish gains water from its environment and must secrete it at a high rate.

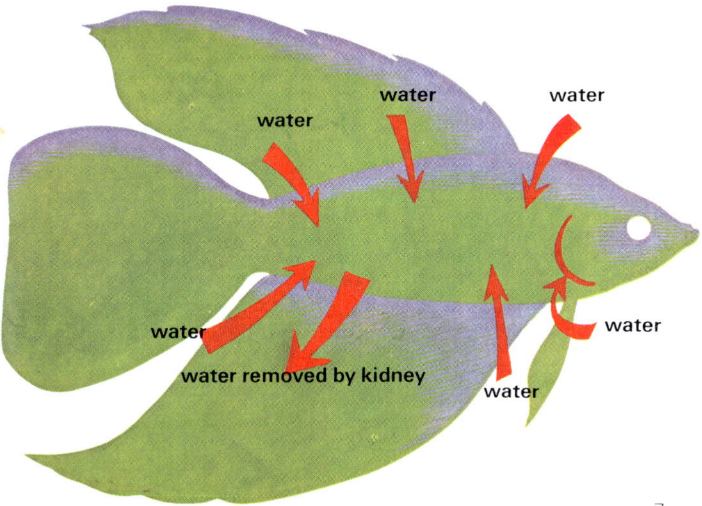

It will now be obvious that we are imposing an unnecessarily large metabolic load on sea aquarium fishes if we maintain their water at too great a salt concentration (of which the specific gravity is a measure). The often quoted 'normal' specific gravity reading of 1·025 should be a *maximum* level, and most fishes are happier in water of specific gravity 1·018 to 1·022, [measured at a water temperature of 75°F (24°C)].

Another difference between seawater and freshwater fishes is caused by a difference in the quality of the two types of water. In the tropics, where most freshwater aquarium fishes come from, there are large seasonal variations in water quality caused by the annual dry season-rainy season cycle. Periodically, and usually during the rains, relatively large amounts of organic and inorganic matter are washed into waterways inhabited by such fishes as barbs, characins, cichlids, rasboras and anabantids. These cycles of high pollution-low pollution have been going on for many hundreds of millions of years,

(*Below* and *opposite*) Four species of fishes from the same area of the same reef exhibit the typical spectacular coloration of coral-reef animals.

Yellow Skunk Clownfish

Regal Tang

Fire Clownfish

Green Parrot Wrasse

so that freshwater fishes have evolved compensating metabolic processes and are thus able to survive this environmental variation without too many ill-effects.

The coral reef, on the other hand, regarding both physical and chemical conditions, is (after the abyssal depths) probably the most stable habitat on this planet. The changes of environmental water on the reef are so relatively minute and slow in occurrence that the true reef-dwellers, for example the butterfly fishes (*Chaetodon* spp), have not evolved metabolic versatility to cope with sudden and drastic changes in water quality. This difference alone between seawater and freshwater fishes accounts for the anomalous experiences of many experienced freshwater aquarists, who, having been successful in maintaining a small, for example, 10 gallon (45 litre) freshwater aquarium, come to grief when attempting to maintain marine life-forms in the same tank. In such a small

The Fire Clownfish defending spawn on a rock face. Some reef fishes will spawn in aquaria but the fry do not usually survive.

body of water, changes in water quality that inevitably occur with water-ageing, take place more rapidly than the marine organisms can adapt. I would never recommend anyone to make a start in marine aquarium keeping with a tank which is smaller than 20 gallons (90 litres). Ideally one should obtain the largest tank which either the size of one's house or one's wallet will permit.

The next difference between the two groups of fishes is one for which there is no widely accepted answer. Why are coral-reef animals so much more spectacularly coloured than freshwater animals? All the fishes shown on the previous two pages come from the same area of the same reef surrounding one of the Philippine Islands, and the riotous colour variation is self-apparent. The theory that the coloration serves as camouflage would never be suggested by anyone with normal colour vision who has swum on a reef. The colours make the fishes stand out like 'sore thumbs'. Perhaps the most likely

A Cleaner Wrasse removing parasites from a Regal Tang. A number of fishes on the reef provide this curious social service.

explanation is the most recent one, i.e., the coloration ensures that, despite the enormous quantity of life on the reef and the striking similarity in shape and size of fishes of the same genera, members of the same species can still recognize each other at mating times. This would prevent the catastrophe of many matings producing sterile hybrids as a result of inter-specific crossing. Such crosses would obviously be of negative species-survival value.

The experimentally minded marine aquarist might like to attempt to verify or discount this hypothesis by devising experiments, which, if suitably controlled would indicate whether or not coral fishes possess colour vision. Any good book on animal behaviour and intelligence would suggest experimental methods requiring little apparatus.

This section would not be complete without mention of the astonishing behaviour of quite a few fishes on the reef which pick parasites from the bodies of other larger fishes.

Although this kindly action (not altogether selfless, since the 'cleaner' has a good meal from the parasites removed), is found on dry land in several instances, for example, tick birds cleaning the teeth of crocodiles, there is, as far as I know, no comparable behaviour among freshwater fishes.

This unusual behaviour finds its most frequent expression in the attentions almost incessantly paid by the small, very pretty Cleaner Wrasse (*Labroides dimidiatus*) to almost any larger fish which it feels may be harbouring parasites. However, almost all fishes of the family Chaetodontidae, and especially the Wimple fish (*Heniochus acuminatus*), display this 'cleaning' behaviour as juveniles and in isolated instances it may even be carried through into early adulthood.

At any given temperature, the oxygen saturation of sea water is far less than that of fresh water. Thus aeration in the marine aquarium is essential to satisfy the oxygen requirements of the occupants.

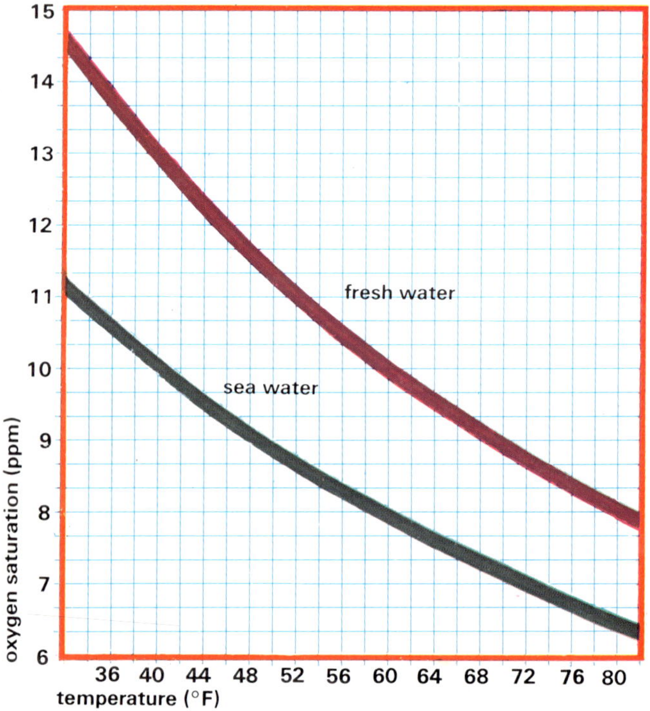

THE RIGHT CONDITIONS

Synthetic or natural sea water?

It would appear to be self-evident that any medium in which an animal has evolved for the last few hundred million years will be the best medium to be used in a life-support system for that animal. It therefore follows that real sea water should be the best medium in which to culture marine organisms, provided that it is properly cured prior to use. Unfortunately, sea water taken straight from the sea immediately begins to undergo many complex and incompletely understood biochemical changes. Massive populations of bacteria come and go in cycles, phytoplankton and zooplankton deteriorate in vitality and eventually die, thus further exacerbating the bacteria problem.

Correct curing entails storing the sea water in a non-toxic container at low temperature, between 45 and 50°F (7 to 10°C), in total darkness for four to six months. At the end of this period the clear liquid only should be syphoned off for use in the aquarium. This is exactly what is done at Brighton Aquarium, where a 250,000 gallon (1,125,000 litre) underground storage tank is used for water settling and curing. However, few marine aquarists can avail themselves of such facilities, and in any event, since formulating the salt mix now sold as 'Synthetica', I have never used natural sea water in my aquaria. During these latter years the results I have obtained with synthetic sea water have been infinitely greater than those enjoyed in my 'real sea water' days. I can only suggest that the differences in results may be due to the fact that even long-cured natural sea water may still contain exceptionally durable pathogens (disease-producing organisms), whereas freshly prepared synthetic sea water is, of course, sterile.

Aeration

An air pump is an absolutely essential item in a marine aquarium. The oxygen requirements and equally important, the intolerance of carbon dioxide levels of coral-reef animals, are approximately 250 per cent greater and 50 per cent lower respectively, than comparable freshwater animals. In view of these requirements it is imperative that aeration and filtration systems are kept at the maximum possible levels for twenty-four hours each day and must never be switched off for more than a few minutes.

Filtration

Unless one is courageous enough to be considering a sea aquarium set up on the 'natural system' which will be described later, another essential item for one's tank is a filter. We can differentiate between the two sorts of filtration as follows:–

(i) **Mechanical filtration** This term will be used in the text to refer to the removal from the water of individually or collectively visible gross particles of detritus, uneaten food, excreta, bacteria and protozoa etc. This type of filtration is usually sufficient to ensure water clarity but if this becomes a recurrent problem, effective filtration of a second type is

The oxygen tension of foul sea water is considerably less, at a given temperature, than that of clean sea water. Filtration systems keep aquarium water clean and therefore at maximum oxygen tension.

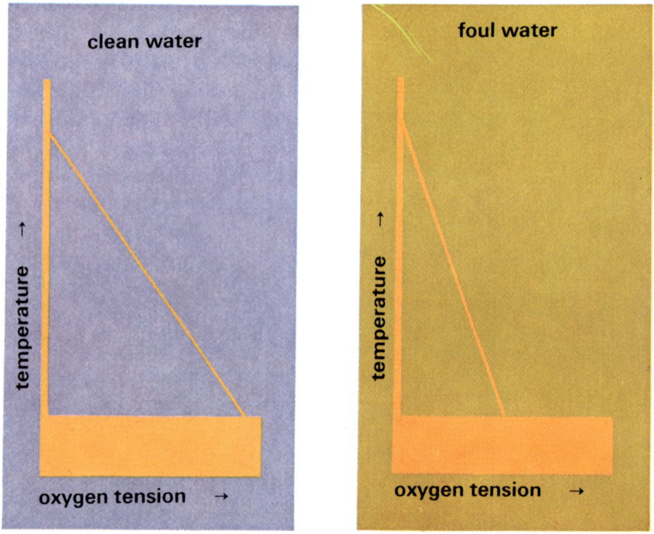

necessary to ensure clear water in the aquarium.

(ii) **Biochemical filtration** This term refers to the removal from solution, or the de-toxification of organic chemicals in solution which could give rise to the large bacteria and plankton counts which cause persistent cloudy water.

The toxic chemicals which may be present in the sea water in the aquarium are proteinaceous matter, albumenoid compounds, ionized and un-ionized ammonia and nitrite (not to be confused with less-toxic nitrate) salts. If they are present in excessive quantities they may cause the premature deaths of all aquarium animals. Strictly speaking, nitrites are not organic chemicals and neither is ammonia in any form but they are included here because they are intermediate products in the process of bacterial breakdown of organic matter.

Highly poisonous organic matter may be introduced into the water in any one of a variety of ways as follows:–

Particles in the water are trapped in a filter medium by mechanical filtration (*left*). Toxic chemicals are removed from solution or converted into harmless groups by biochemical filtration (*right*).

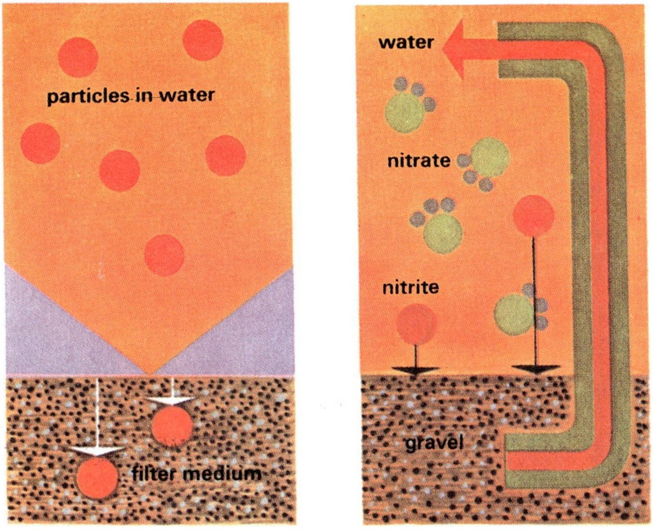

(i) by the use of uncured or inadequately cured corals or shells;
(ii) by the unnoticed death and subsequent decay of an animal or plant in the aquarium;
(iii) by careless overfeeding of the specimens in the sea aquarium, with the inevitable decay of uneaten food in the water;
(iv) by the usage of any decor items which release ammonia or nitrites into the water, such as crushed shells which have not been bleached for several days before use in a filter-bed;
(v) by the addition to the water of inexpertly formulated plant fertilizer solutions.

The whole question of filtration in the sea aquarium is fully treated later on in the book.

Specific gravity

For the non-technical reader it is felt that a slightly more comprehensive treatment of the meaning, measurement and importance of specific gravity than has already been given would be welcomed here. To begin with, specific gravity, unlike most other measurable quantities, has no units of measurement. In other words it is correct to say that aquarium water reads specific gravity 1·021, but neither necessary nor strictly correct to say that aquarium water reads specific

A hydrometer enables the aquarist to read off the specific gravity of his aquarium water.

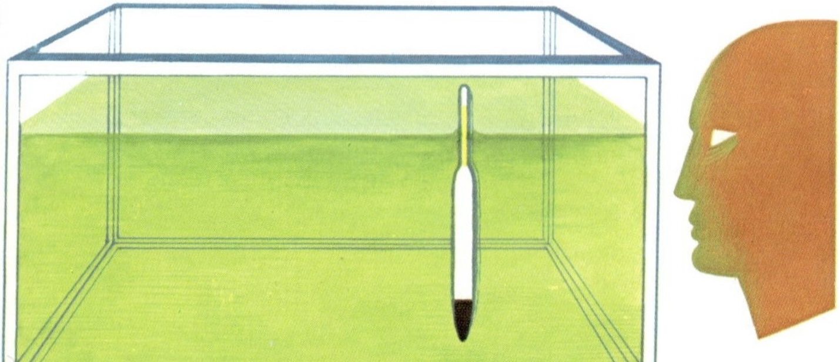

gravity 1·021 gm/cc. The units 'grams per cubic centimetre' are not needed since the density of pure water at 39°F (4°C) is exactly 1 gm/cc, and the specific gravity of a substance is the number of times that that substance *is heavier than an equal volume of pure water at a temperature of 39°F (4°C).* What we are really saying therefore is that aquarium water is 1·021 times heavier than the same volume of pure water at a temperature of 39°F (4°C).

The difference in weight between sea water and the same volume of pure, fresh water is obviously caused by the salts that are present in the sea water. The more salt added, the higher the specific gravity of the solution becomes and vice versa. For high accuracy, it is necessary to relate the specific gravity reading to the temperature of the sample when it was measured. This is because exactly the same sea water would give a lower specific gravity reading at say 80°F (26°C) than it would at 70°F (21°C). This will not concern the marine aquarist possessing a *hydrometer*. This is an instrument used to measure specific gravity which is calibrated for the average temperature at which marine life-forms from the tropics are normally kept.

Acidity and alkalinity

The *p*H number is another 'unitless' index number used to indicate the acidity and alkalinity of liquids. Fresh sea water usually gives a *p*H value of 8·0 to 8·3. As will be seen from the diagrammatic scale overleaf this means that sea water in good condition is slightly alkaline. The *p*H of aquarium water is usually measured by the marine aquarist on a colour scale as shown. A small amount of a chemical reagent, known as an indicator solution, is added to a measured volume of the water and the resulting colour change is compared with standard colours. This is usually sufficiently accurate but for really accurate measurement a *p*H meter is used.

Finally, it should be stated that provided the readings of specific gravity and *p*H are within the normal parameters (specific gravity 1·019 to 1·025 and *p*H 8·0 to 8·3), the actual value recorded is not nearly as important as the fact that *any changes made in these parameters should occur at the slowest possible rate.*

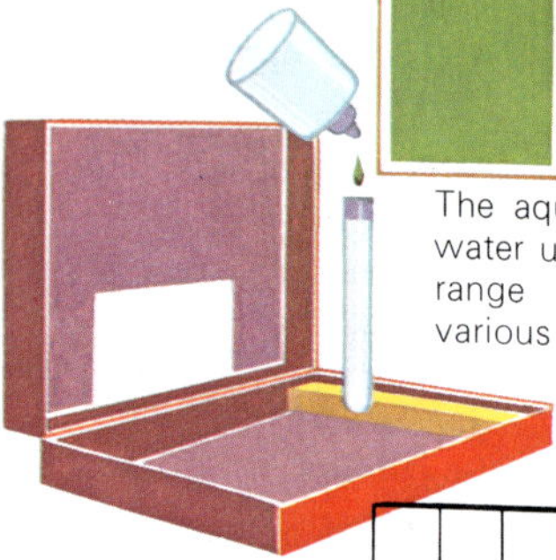

The aquarist can check the alkalinity of his sea water using a *p*H kit (*left*). Indicator dyes give a range of colours (*above*) corresponding to various *p*H values.

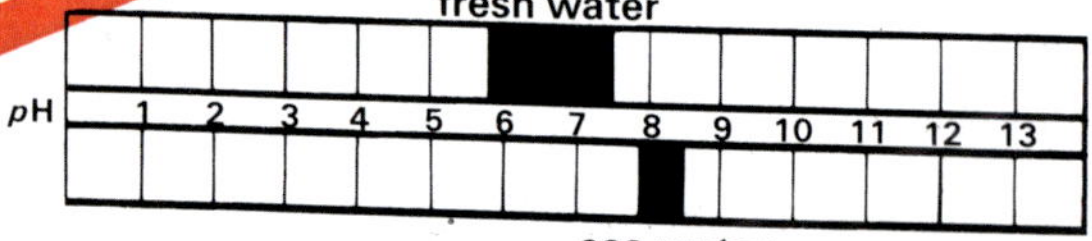

The *p*H of fresh water varies over a wider range than that of sea water. Fresh water is slightly acid, sea water slightly alkaline. (*p*H 7 = neutral).

Lighting

The amount of lighting necessary to illuminate a marine aquarium is an open question. Some aquarists may wish to maintain the decor and refuge items in the aquarium, for example corals, shells and rocks, in the state of virgin cleanliness that they were purchased, and they will be advised to keep the illumination to the lowest level that permits easy viewing of the aquarium's occupants. The reason for this is that in natural sea water and a well-formulated synthetic sea water, there are salts present such as nitrates and phosphates and traces of certain metals (potassium, boron, iron, magnesium and others) and non-metals (sulphur and iodine) that are vital nutrients stimulating plant growth. With lighting at a high intensity, approaching that of light falling on the reef, all decor items within the aquarium quickly become coated with a patina of delicately shaded green and brown algae.

Other aquarists have no objection to such growths and to get a rich and more natural covering of this algae it is almost impossible to have too much light in a marine aquarium. The limiting factors, however, are usually overheating of the aquarium water which causes the oxygen tension to fall drastically with immediate effect, and crippling electricity bills, which have a less immediate but equally disturbing effect.

Most readers will know that white light is made up of red, orange, yellow, green, blue, indigo and violet light mixed together. What many may not know however, is that these components of white light have varying abilities to penetrate water. Light from the red end of the spectrum has less ability to penetrate sea water than light from the blue end. However, green plants require more red light than blue light, whereas brown and red algae require more bluey-green light than red light.

Fluorescent light has a greater blue than red content (*left*) while incandescent light has a greater red than blue content (*right*).

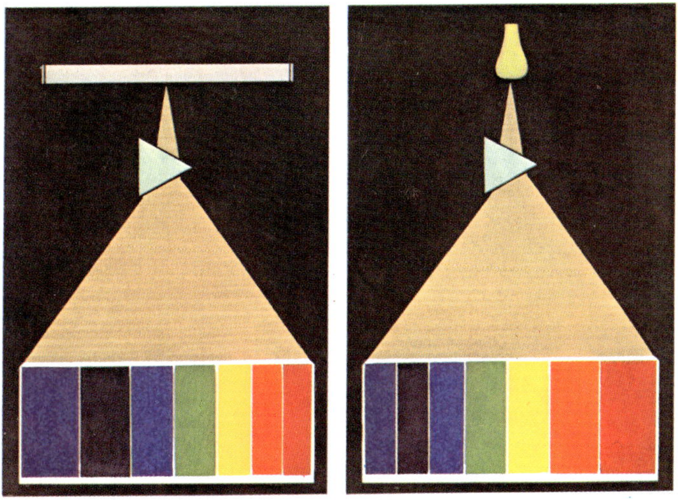

Obviously then, in choosing the correct lighting for the job, we must examine the different qualities of light emitted from available light sources. Incandescent (tungsten or carbon filament) bulbs emit a light which has a greater red content than the normal fluorescent tube, although colour-corrected fluorescent tubes are available which go a long way towards correcting this chromatic inbalance. An advantage of fluorescent tubes over incandescent light sources is that, in the former, almost all the electricity used is converted into light, whereas in the latter a good proportion of it is wasted as heat. Conversely, the initial cost of a fluorescent tube and the control equipment needed to run it is high, whereas a light-bulb and holder cost little.

There are two compromise solutions to this problem:–

(i) an incandescent striplight and a normal white fluorescent tube;

(ii) a colour-corrected fluorescent tube and a normal white fluorescent tube.

Both, of course, should be fitted in a correctly designed hood as shown.

The aquarium hood should carry the light source at the front of the tank (*below*), so that the occupants are viewed by reflected light. Transmitted light from the rear of the tank (*bottom*) will affect the colours of the fishes.

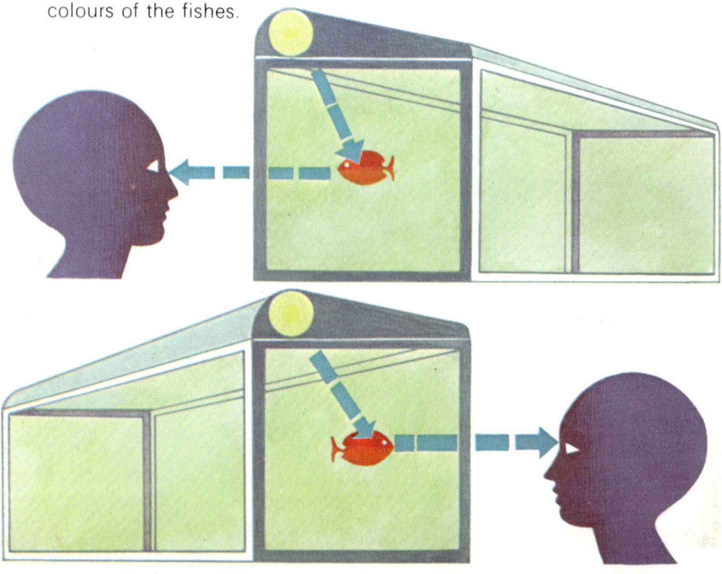

THE RIGHT EQUIPMENT

Choosing the tank

Basically, an aquarium is a strong container which allows us to see, and therefore enjoy our miniature coral reef in the home. Unfortunately, there are so many variations on the apparently simple 'strong container' theme that we must first examine the special qualities that the marine aquarist will expect of his tank, and then arrange the available types in order of increasing suitability for our purposes.

Sea water, whether natural or synthetic, is extremely corrosive. It contains many chemicals which readily attack all metals (except noble metals) and marine quality stainless steels. It is obvious then that if any type of metal-framed tank is used, the frame must be protected from contact with the water by some insulating layer of inert material. In the early days the only way a pioneer marine aquarist could obtain an effective protection was to very carefully paint the angle-iron frame of the tank. This is still the cheapest way of preparing a marine aquarium provided that care is

A metal-framed glass tank can be used as a marine aquarium providing the angle-iron framework is painted and all the internal seams are sealed.

taken when the tank is in commission, to ensure that this vital layer of paint is not scratched, thus exposing the underlying steel to attacks of rust. This will be of interest to the established freshwater aquarist who may be considering converting one of his old tanks for use as a sea aquarium. It is strongly recommended that in addition to carrying out top quality paintwork on the frame, such a conversion should also include the sealing of all internal seams of the aquarium with an approved silicone sealant. This is necessary for any conventional putty-glazed tank, because many glazing compounds used are toxic to marine animals. In any event, treating a tank in this way renders it permanently leak-proof even after many years when the putty has dried, cracked and lost its adhesive qualities. Even if such a tank should rust, the effect of corrosion is unlikely to kill the fishes.

Other variations of protected metal-framed tanks are the P.V.C. (or preferably nylon-coated) iron-framed tank, the polyester or epoxy-coated iron-framed tank, and more recently, the anodised aluminium-framed tank. In the latter case, serious aluminium poisoning of the water will result if the anodised surface is scratched on any part of the top frame making contact with the water.

Next in order of suitability are all-plastic aquaria. These

Alternatively, the metal frame can be protected by a nylon or plastic coat.

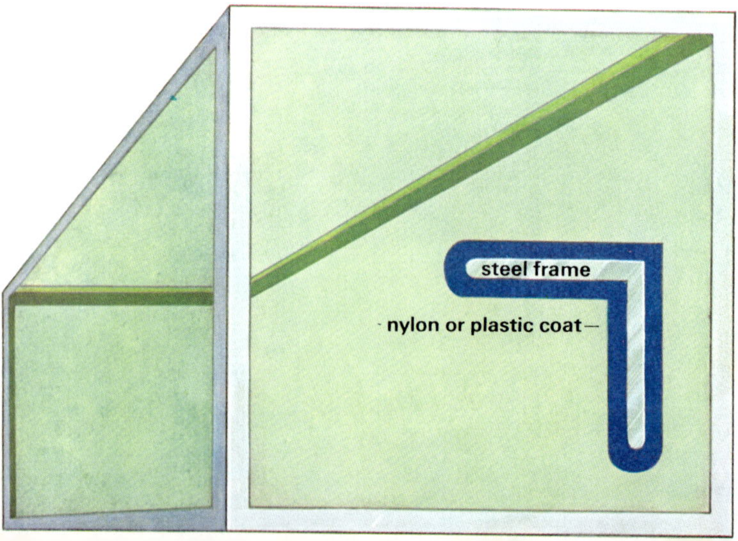

are usually made of acrylic plastics like Perspex, which in the case of small tanks up to 36 × 12 × 12 in (90 × 30 × 30 cm), are mass-produced by vacuum-forming. Larger units are fabricated from plastic sheets. Their advantages are low weight and in the case of the small mass-produced units, low cost. The larger units are hand-made and tend to be rather expensive, and all types share the common defect of losing transparency with age, due to minute scratches which are almost inevitably incurred when removing abrasive diatomaceous growths from the front 'glass'. However, these tanks are non-toxic and not prone to corrosion.

With the recent development of silicone rubber adhesive sealants previously referred to, it has now become possible to literally glue sheets of glass together to produce a surprisingly strong, if fragile-looking, cheap, non-toxic and non-corrodible container.

The marine quality stainless steel-framed tanks are placed next in this list of available aquaria. Owing to the cost of such high grade steel, these tanks are never cheap. They are strong, non-toxic, non-corrodible (providing the steel is truly marine quality) and, if properly made, will probably outlive ten tanks from the preceding categories. The reasons they are not at the head of the list are that they are enormously

Glass-fronted fibreglass tanks have been designed specially for use as marine aquaria.

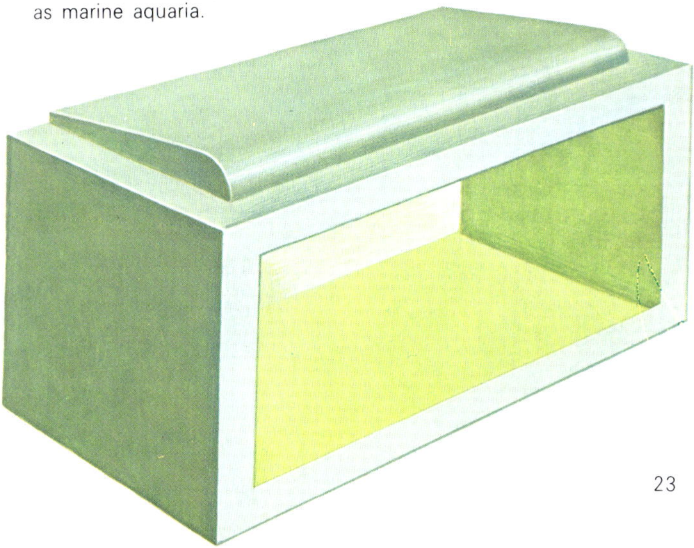

expensive, size for size with the next tank, they are very heavy, and lastly, some people find their somewhat flashy appearance objectionable.

Finally, we come to the most recent development of all, the fibreglass reinforced plastic tank, with a true glass front bonded to the plastic frame with silicone rubber sealant. In this tank, all but one of all the desirable qualities are embodied as follows:-

(i) low weight;
(ii) non-toxic;
(iii) non-corrodible;
(iv) good appearance;
(v) high heat retention;
(vi) can be made in almost any colour or finish;
(vii) high strength, i.e., heavy decor objects can be used.

The discerning reader will have noticed that the omitted desirable quality is 'low cost'. These aquaria are hand-made at the moment and are consequently expensive, but plans

A 'built-in' marine aquarium forms a fascinating decorative asset to a room. An all-glass tank is shown (*left*).

are already to hand for their mass production.

Such are the available containers. Not every reader will agree to the sequence of desirability used above but it is hoped that a sufficiently unbiased appraisal of the relative attributes of each tank has been given.

Heaters and thermostats

It is almost impossible to purchase a poorly made British heater or thermostat these days, and even the teething problems experienced by the manufacturers of the latest innovation – the combined heater and thermostat – are now solved. There is not therefore the question of which brand of equipment to purchase but rather a choice of the type of heating equipment to serve one's requirements best.

In choosing a heater the major problem is one of matching the wattage of the instrument to the volume of water to be heated, taking into account of course, the ambient temperature of the room in which the sea aquarium is to be sited. This is a most important consideration, for an aquarium located in an unheated room will obviously require more heating in a given period of time than would the same aquarium in a modern, centrally heated room. A good general rule to apply is one 100 watt heater for an aquarium volume of 20 gallons (90 litres) in a normally heated room, or one 150 watt heater for the same volume in an unheated or poorly heated room. This is a lower wattage to volume ratio than many authors have suggested but I shall justify these figures shortly.

The choice of a thermostat is a little more difficult owing to the great variety of these instruments now available. Generally speaking, if money is no object, I would advise the purchase of an external fitting clip-on thermostat of superior manufacture with a wattage rating up to 2,000 watts. Such an instrument would be able to cope with the temperature regulation of up to twenty tanks, each with 100 watt heaters, assuming that the novice aquarist becomes thoroughly absorbed with his hobby. If the beginner is certain that he will not become quite so involved then a similar design but cheaper external thermostat rated at 500 watts will give adequate reserve. For the iron-willed, certain that they will never have more than the one sea aquarium, a small, moderately priced 200 watt internal fitting instrument enclosed in a glass-tube will be adequate.

The reason why a slightly lower than normal wattage to volume ratio has been suggested can now be explained. The only parts of the heater-thermostat combination liable to wear are the platinum-coated contact breakers in the thermostat. It follows therefore, that the less these points have to open and close the better. A low wattage heater will of course have to stay on longer to produce a unit quantity of heat but it must not be assumed that more electricity is consumed. A large wattage heater running for a short time uses just as much electricity as a low wattage heater running for a longer time.

If you decide to use a separate heater and thermostat, you must ensure that the electrical connection between the two instruments is well insulated with P.V.C. tape and/or sealed with silicone sealer. Salt water is a good conductor of electricity and finds its way into the least convenient places.

The ideal means of heating a sea aquarium is with a combined

A combined heater and thermostat (*below*) and an external fitting clip-on thermostat (*bottom*).

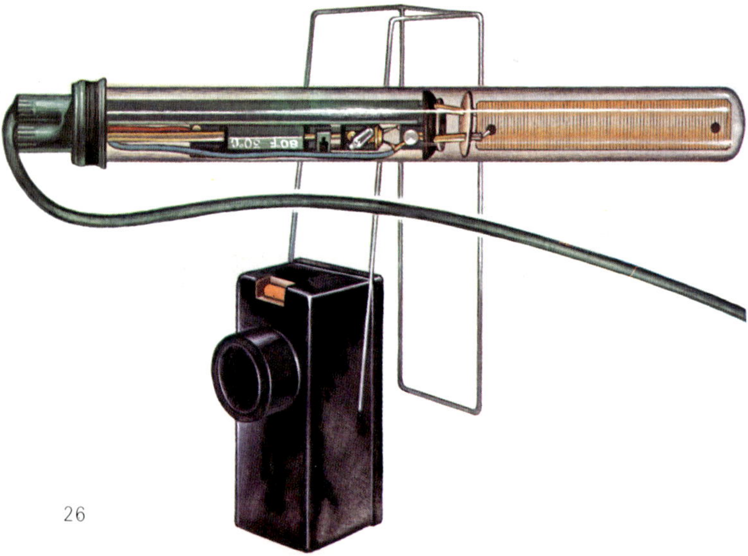

heater and thermostat, since with these instruments there is only one lead carrying mains current and this, fitted with a plug, goes straight into a power point, which should be above water level if possible.

Thermometers

An all-glass thermometer is ideal for the sea aquarium and should be fixed to the inside glass surface of one of the aquarium sides as unobtrusively as possible. Such instruments are generally attached to the glass by means of a synthetic rubber (or non-toxic plastic) disc. It is particularly important that the thermometer used in the sea aquarium has no metallic parts exposed to the salt water.

It is worth paying a little extra for a truly accurate thermometer, as many of the cheaper models of oriental manufacture frequently show an error of plus or minus 5°F (3°C). This is not important of course if the deviation from accuracy is linear, i.e., it is constant throughout the range of temperature readings. In this case one compares the defective instrument's reading with that of a high accuracy instrument and noting the inaccuracy, compensates accordingly whenever taking a reading. The keen marine aquarist will soon get into the

Separate heater (*below*) and thermostat (*bottom*) and an all-glass thermometer with adhesive disc (*left*).

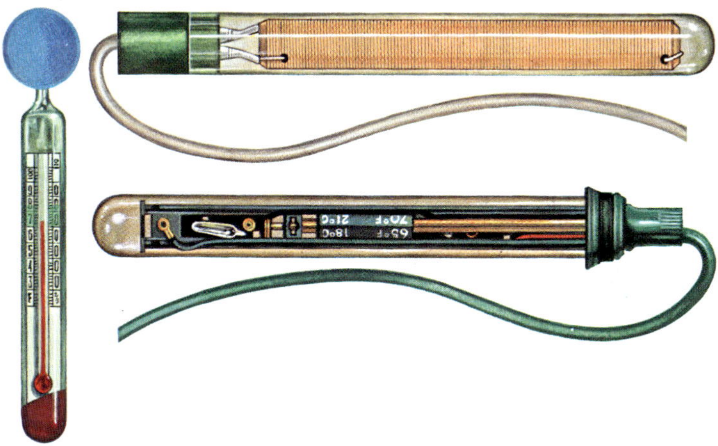

habit of checking the temperature of the water every time he feeds his animals. For the Mediterranean sea aquarium the water should be kept in the range 68–72°F (20–22°C), whereas a sea aquarium for tropical life-forms requires a water temperature of 74–78°F (24-26°C).

Air pumps

Two types of pumps are available to the marine aquarist:-

(i) **Vibrator pumps** These units are undoubtedly the cheapest and most maintenance-free of the air supply equipment under consideration. A vibrator pump requires no oiling, is fairly silent, delivers a very smooth, i.e., 'non-lumpy' supply of air and gives very good value in terms of cubic inches of air delivered per watt of electricity consumed. The most powerful units rate at about thirty watts and so will consume one unit of power only after they have been run non-stop for thirty hours. It is important to keep the small cotton wool air filter clean, since an accumulation of dust under the rubber flap-valves, which control the admission and removal of air through the valve block, seriously reduces the air output of the pump.

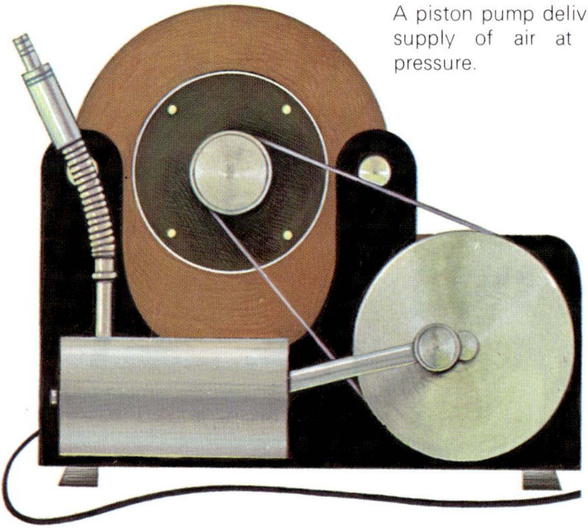

A piston pump delivers a smooth supply of air at considerable pressure.

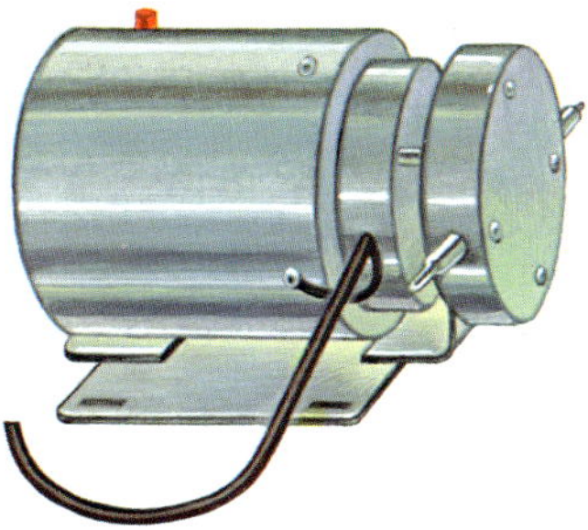

Very efficient high-powered rotary pumps will soon be available to marine aquarists.

(ii) **Piston pumps** Although considerably more expensive, piston pumps have the advantage of delivering more air at greater pressure than average priced vibrator pumps. The earlier piston pumps were of all-metal construction and needed frequent lubrication of moving parts but modern units usually make use of self-lubricating plastics. This has removed the need for frequent attention and brought about a reduction in noise level.

We may see presently the appearance of high powered rotary blowers in miniature which should provide greater volumes of air in unit time than air pumps currently available, although the pressure at which the air is delivered is unlikely to be as great.

Water filters

Broadly speaking, all currently available filtration equipment may be placed into one of the following categories:–

(i) **Power filters** As the name suggests, the water passes through the filter media in these units under power. The power is supplied by an electric motor, suitably isolated from contact with the salt water, which drives a plastic impeller fan.

The advantage of these units is that they move large volumes of water in a short space of time which is exactly what is required for marine fishes. Furthermore, the power available means that the water can be forced through the minute inter-fibre spaces created by packing man-made fibre 'wool' into the filter chamber. In addition to the high degree of *mechanical filtration* (see pages 14 and 15) conferred by this means, some degree of *chemical filtration* can be obtained as one can also place highly activated charcoal in the filter chamber. High activity charcoal has the ability to adsorb certain organic gases and even low molecular weight organic solids in the water. It will also remove from solution the phenol-related yellowish coloured compounds so characteristic of old sea water, and so acts as a decolorizer.

(ii) **Filters utilizing airlifts** Several types of airlift operated filters are discussed below, but in terms of biochemical filtration efficiency, *the undergravel or subsand filter is the filtration system of paramount importance to all marine aquarists.*

Once the gravel covering such a filter has 'ripened', i.e., it contains enormous populations of aerobic nitrifying bacteria, it is almost impossible to foul the water in a sea aquarium filtered in this way. These bacteria are able to oxidize the organic wastes produced as excreta by the marine animals as well as the decomposition products from uneaten foods, into relatively safe nitrate salts. These nitrates are then utilized by algae and diatoms in the synthesis of plant proteins. In the near

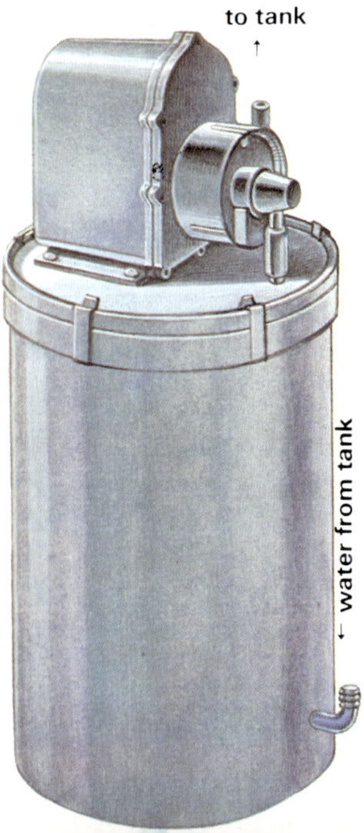

A power filter (*left*) and an undergravel filter utilizing an air-lift (*right*) provide both mechanical and biochemical filtration.

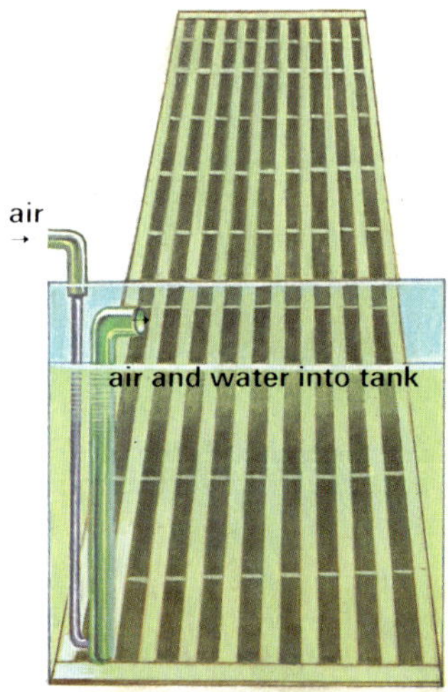

future, de-ionizing resins will be developed which will be capable of the selective removal from solution of the organic toxins that cause discomfort and even death in marine animals, without profoundly affecting the *p*H of sea water. These resins will be used most effectively in a power filter but it is doubtful whether, for sheer low cost, long life, safety, and the absence of maintenance, they will ever replace the undergravel filter as a means of de-toxification of sea water.

In contrasting the rival merits of the power filter and the high efficiency seawater undergravel filter, the most apparent difference is one of cost. A good power filter is costly and needs frequent servicing with expensive new filter materials. A good undergravel filter is cheaply made by the handyman or can be purchased at relatively low cost. A power filter is operated by a complex electric motor whereas an undergravel filter is operated by an air pump, the only likely repairs to which are the annual replacement of the inexpensive rubber diaphragm. The undergravel filter does not remove the microscopic plankton life-forms from the water needed by such filter-feeding invertebrates as tubeworms, corals and sponges, whereas the power filter does do this. On the other hand, charcoal is easily used in a power filter and this is very helpful in sea water management.

To summarize, if the prospective marine aquarist can afford only one filter for his aquarium, he should buy or make a powerful undergravel filter. If on the other hand, money is not an important consideration, and he wishes to study only marine fishes and non filter-feeding invertebrates such as anemones, crabs and shrimps, sea urchins and cowries etc., then he should purchase *both* an undergravel filter and a power filter. For the vast majority of middle income marine aquarists, a good compromise is a powerful undergravel filter and one external or internal fitting airlift operated filter, of the types described next, filled with high-activity charcoal.

Bubble-up external filters These are modestly priced and yet surprisingly efficient little external filters. They can be filled with charcoal and nylon 'wool' and are thus capable of giving both the decolorizing action and higher degree of mechanical filtration lacking with an undergravel filter. They

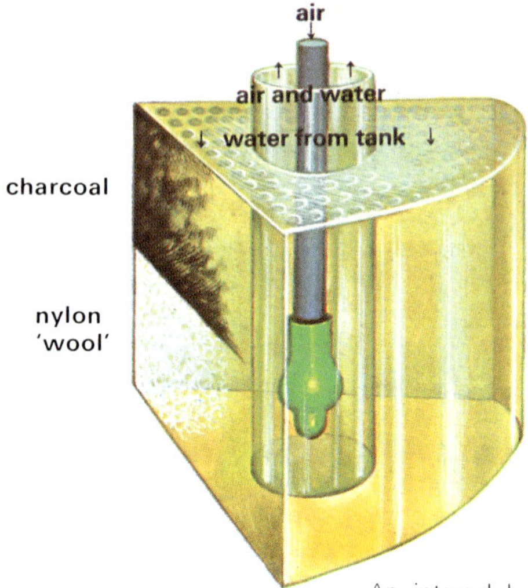

An internal bubble-up filter fits into a bottom corner of the tank.

are operated by a small and cheap air pump and so have neither the high cost, complexity or need for frequent maintenance that is necessary with the motor-driven filter.

Bubble-up internal filters These very effective little units have the advantage of being easy to maintain. Their unnatural appearance within a sea aquarium can be offset by location behind a piece of rock, shell or coral. For the average 20–100 gallons (90–450 litres) tank such a filter, filled with marine-grade charcoal ('seacoal') to absorb toxic phenols, together with an undergravel filter provides the optimum seawater management system.

Surface-fitting corner filters Exactly the same criticisms apply to these filters as to the last described, except that these units are even more difficult to hide.

Filter media Generally speaking, the only filter medium that is used with an undergravel filter is carefully graded gravel and preferably a layer of *p*H buffering material of suitable size, such as crushed coral, oyster shell or coral-sand. With all the other types of filters discussed above, filter media can be highly activated charcoal, nylon floss and de-ionizing resins. In addition, a new filter medium has recently appeared on the

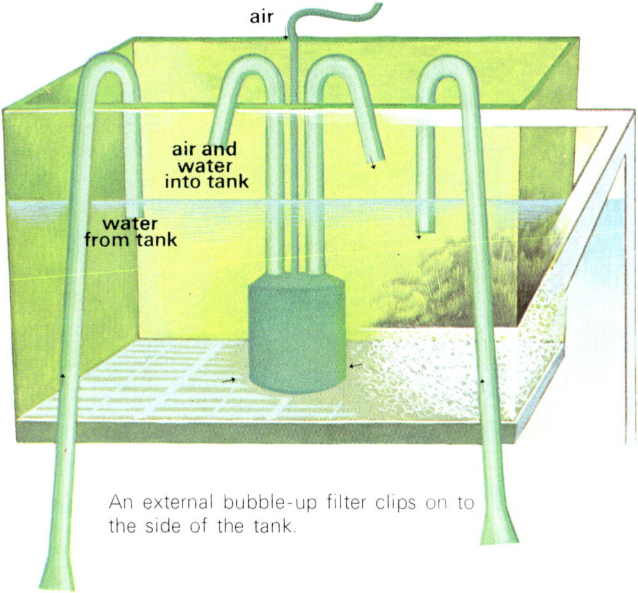

An external bubble-up filter clips on to the side of the tank.

market for use in power filters only. This has an interstitial lattice-work which is so fine that not even bacteria nor motile algae can pass. This material is called diatonaceous earth.

The ozonizer

The oxygen we breathe is made up of molecules containing two atoms, i.e., the normal molecular state of oxygen. However, if oxygen gas is passed through a very high tension electric field, the atoms re-group into threes, i.e., they form the rare and unstable tri-atomic molecule called ozone. This poisonous gas is one of the most powerful oxidizing agents known to man and is a potent bactericide. It is of tremendous value to the aquarist preferring a practically sterile tank (see page 38) because it is his only means of oxidizing ammonia to nitrites and nitrites to the harmless nitrates. To aquarists preferring more natural marine systems it is of value because of its prophylactic and therapeutic value as a bactericide, although the gas must be used with caution to avoid the lethal effects on nitrifying, gravel-dwelling bacteria. There are many other positive values which ozone has in the marine aquarium but the reader must not assume that he will not succeed as a marine aquarist without an ozonizer. Nothing could be further from the truth.

The protein skimmer

It has long been common knowledge among specialists in sewage treatment that if minute air bubbles foam through water with a high organic waste content (such as raw sewage or sea water fouled by inexpert feeding or dead animals), many of the organic chemicals responsible for this pollution will migrate to the surface of the air bubbles. When the bubbles reach the surface they congregate to form a stable foam. The greater the degree of organic pollution in the water the more stable the foam. The beginner will do well to realize that one of the earliest symptoms of incipient fouling is the presence of just such a foam on the surface of the water. If some means could be devised of collecting this foam and allowing it to collapse into liquid which could then be thrown away, fouling of the aquarium water could be prevented. The diagram opposite shows just such an apparatus, usually called a protein skimmer. To the aquarist possessing a high turn-over rate undergravel filter it is of academic interest only because the nitrifying bacteria living in the gravel of the filter will prevent all but the most persistent pollution.

The ultra-violet sterilizer

This is a device which is operated efficiently only by a power filter. Water from the power filter delivery tube circulates around a source of ultra-violet radiation. This radiation is lethal in even small doses to bacteria and protozoa responsible for diseases in aquarium fishes, but unfortunately is equally lethal to the vast majority of other planktonic organisms, many of which are used as food by filter-feeders. As a prophylactic device, i.e., a means of preventing disease, such a unit may have its uses, but it will obviously be unable to prevent a disease if the reproductive rate of the pathogen is faster than the turn-over rate of the power filter supplying the sterilizer with water, as is often the case.

A protein skimmer (*left*) and an ultra-violet sterilizer (*right*)

foam collapses to liquid
tank
water from tank in
movement of water
movement of minute air bubbies
air lift

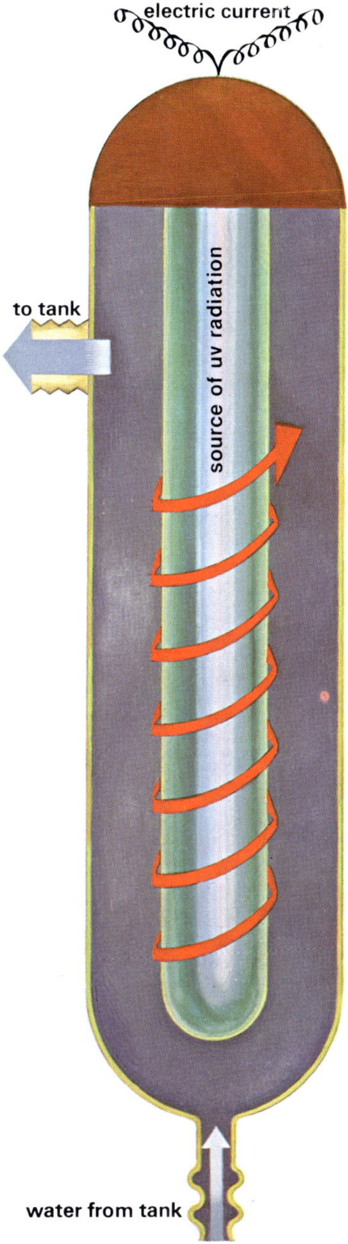
electric current
to tank
source of uv radiation
water from tank

CREATING A MARINE AQUARIUM

The natural system

The natural system of maintaining a marine aquarium is an attempt to create as closely as possible a miniature environment identical in every important respect to the living coral reef. This system eschews all artificial aids to seawater management except one, and this exception means that the natural system is not in fact, truly natural. We have already seen that few marine animals will tolerate stagnant sea water. Recognizing this fact as inescapable, the aquarist maintaining his tank on

An established natural system marine aquarium.

the natural system always uses at least aeration as a means of creating some movement in his sea aquarium water.

The system was originally called the natural system because its adherents refuse the assistance of all man-made filtration aids, relying simply on the living coral-reef filter-feeders such as sponges, living corals, tubeworms and bryozoa to clean the water, i.e., to effect mechanical filtration. Biochemical filtration in such an aquarium is carried out only by the nitrifying bacteria coating every solid surface inside the unit making contact with the salt water. Since there is no undergravel filtration, a thick gravel bed cannot be used because there is the danger that uneaten food and excreta may decompose anaerobically in the gravel to produce poisonous gases such as hydrogen sulphide and methane. Without a thick gravel bed with an enormous surface area available for populations of nitrifying bacteria, the nitrifying potential of the tank is very low.

The foremost and original exponent of this system was Lee Chin Eng of Djakarta, Indonesia. Unfortunately, what many of the original students of his method in Europe did not realize was that should anything go wrong in such a biosystem, for example accidental overfeeding or an unnoticed death, the nitrification potential is so minute that massive and unmanageable pollution is the swift result. In a short time all the animals in such a sea aquarium are dead.

Setting up such a sea aquarium is simplicity itself because the only items of equipment needed inside the tank are a heater and thermostat and an air-stone or wooden diffuser block. All manner of 'living stones', i.e., pieces of coral rock heavily encrusted with invertebrate animals and various algae, are grouped in the aquarium to suit the aesthetic sensitivities of the aquarist. Various larger invertebrates of sessile or semi-sessile nature are then strategically placed in the tank. These can include anemones, live coral heads, tubeworms, clams and sponges. Next, various algae and higher marine plants such as eelgrass are sited and lastly the motile invertebrates such as starfishes, sea urchins, nudibranchs, cowries and conches, crayfishes, prawns, shrimps and crabs etc., are added. After allowing a few days for the system to settle down, the fishes can be added.

The semi-natural system

I am convinced that the semi-natural system is the most economical and most successful method of seawater management. This system has been successfully elaborated since originally conceived in 1962 (see 'The New Seaquarium System' by G. F. Cox), but basically the idea remains centred around a high turn-over rate undergravel filter as the most efficient means yet devised of achieving rapid and total nitrification of toxic nitrogenous wastes. Many tropical freshwater aquarists who have attempted to utilize the author's filtration systems in their aquaria have reported very poor plant growth, no doubt caused by the rapid and unnatural circulation of water around the plant roots. However, this does not appear to have any adverse effects on the holdfasts of the marine algae cultured in sea aquaria. The advantages of the semi-natural system are as follows:-

(i) There is a massive nitrification potential making fouling of the water almost impossible after the normal maturation period for the crushed shell/oolitic coralsand filter-bed.

(ii) The aquarist is able to use a bed of gravel natural in appearance, without the danger of anaerobic decomposition of uneaten foods and excreta producing poisonous gases.

(iii) Expensive and ugly pieces of apparatus, such as protein skimmers and power filters, are avoided although the latter may be used if no filter-feeding invertebrates are to be cultured.

(iv) If the airlift of the undergravel filter is brought above water level a considerable degree of water aeration is achieved as a bonus.

(v) The water movement system depends solely on the air supplied by a cheap and trouble-free vibrator-type air pump, although other types of air supply could of course be used with comparable success. The significance of this is that the only thing which can go wrong with a vibrator air pump is a punctured diaphragm, provided that the air filter wool is kept clean. A replacement diaphragm for even the most expensive air pump on the market is very reasonably priced.

Provided due precautions are taken, the considerable advantages conferred by the intelligent use of ozone may be enjoyed using this system. The precautions really consist of ensuring that no ozone bubbles are carried down into the

gravel because these would destroy the valuable nitrifying bacteria coating every particle. To avoid this the airlift should not open above, but as near to the water level as possible.

The clinical system

There is no undergravel filtration in a marine aquarium maintained under the clinical system and so, for the reasons already outlined, there can again be no gravel in the tank.

Algal and diatomaceous growths are not allowed to gain a foothold on any of the corals, shells or rocks in the aquarium and they are prevented from so doing by the periodic bleaching of these items in a commercially prepared bleach solution. The water in the tank is virtually plankton-free because of the twenty-four hour use of power filtration and so no filter-feeding invertebrates can survive. The aquarist is usually committed to a partial or total water change every few months so the nitrate and phosphate levels of the salt water are never high enough to support growth of higher algae such as *Codium, Enteromorpha, Ulva,* etc. However, provided ozone is used at the very high level necessary to maintain the ammonia and nitrite content of the water within tolerable limits, extremely successful results will be obtained by the aquarist.

The only apparatus needed by a clinical system marine aquarist to determine the level of activity of the all-important power filter charcoal is a solid white, flat surface (e.g. a sheet of plastic, white card or tile) and two identical clear glass bottles of at least 8 in (20 cm) in height, such as milk, soft drinks or wine bottles. The taller the bottles the more sensitive the test becomes. The method for conducting the test is as follows:

(i) Fill one bottle with sea water from the aquarium under test, and fill the other with good-quality tap water, rain water or freshly prepared synthetic sea water.

(ii) Stand both bottles side-by-side on the white surface and view them from above in white fluorescent light or daylight, looking down through the full depth of water. If the charcoal still retains some of its toxin-adsorptive capacity there will be no difference in colour between the two samples. Alternatively if the aquarium water is yellowish compared with the control sample, the charcoal is due for renewal.

Remember the more highly active a charcoal the lower its density, and so it tends to float on sea water. Such super-active charcoal should be de-gassed before use by pouring boiling water on it and leaving it to stand for 15–30 minutes.

The tank is usually typified by the use of ion-exchange resin-packed power filters, ozonizers, ultra-violet sterilizers, protein skimmers and 'whiter-than-white' corals. Occasionally the extremist will go to the unforgivable lengths of equipping his sea aquarium with busty mermaids, dyspeptic green plastic frogs, sunken galleons and questing divers and even violet plastic dahlias. Thankfully, many of these aberrations appear to be waning in popularity.

An aquarium maintained under the clinical system

FURNISHING THE MARINE AQUARIUM

The materials available to the marine aquarist for furnishing his aquarium are at least as varied as those available to the freshwater aquarist who is generally limited to plants, rockwork and attractively shaped pieces of dead wood. The marine aquarist has these plus corals of enormous variety of form, sea shells of almost infinite variety of form and colour, and such things as sea fans, gorgonian skeletons, sea urchin tests and not least, the sessile and semi-sessile invertebrate animals themselves such as anemones and tube worms.

The question of how to arrange a given selection of decor objects is of course entirely one of personal choice. Two people will rarely agree on what constitutes beauty. I can only give guide lines as to what pleases me and trust that these views may find favour with the majority of marine aquarists.

Generally speaking, the first thing to do is to choose a striking centre-piece. This may be a giant pink conch shell, a particularly large and splendid coral head or even a large and unusually well-figured piece of rock. Great care should be taken to ensure that this item is not placed in the geometrical centre of the tank. Such an object is better placed one-third to two-fifths of the length of the tank from the end. All the other less significant objects can then be grouped around it to lead up to a 'crescendo'. Always try to group all pieces of the same species of coral together rather than scattering them all over the tank. Keep large shells well to the rear of the tank. Try to avoid purchasing pieces of coral of the same height.

Arrangement of decor items in a well-furnished tank

Instead, buy at least one tall coral, for example branch or elkhorn coral, and use this off-centre, towards the rear of the tank, to create an illusion of vertical depth in the sea aquarium.

Suitable rocks for use in the sea aquarium are Westmorland, Sussex and York stone and most of the Welsh and Cornish slates. There are many other types of rocks with which I have had no experience, and it is suggested that before possibly poisoning a prized collection of animals, any unknown rock-work should be first scrubbed then soaked in salt water for a month, after which *p*H and nitrite tests can be conducted on the water. When positioning rocks and corals, try to keep tall pieces to the rear third of the tank.

When siting decor materials within the tank, bear in mind that almost all the true reef-dwelling species of fishes greatly appreciate the provision of suitably sized hiding places. Among the invertebrates, the octopus, mantis and Boxing Shrimps and crinoids (sea lilies or feather-stars) also welcome similar thoughtfulness.

Shells

Almost all molluscs and particularly the marine molluscs, have the ability to extract certain salts, mostly calcium and magnesium, from sea water and after altering these salts slightly, secrete them as layer upon layer of hard calcareous solids. The resulting completed structure is called the shell and serves to protect the soft and therefore vulnerable tissues within. Eventually the animal which made the shell dies, either from natural causes or because of predation by

Arrangement of decor items in a badly furnished tank

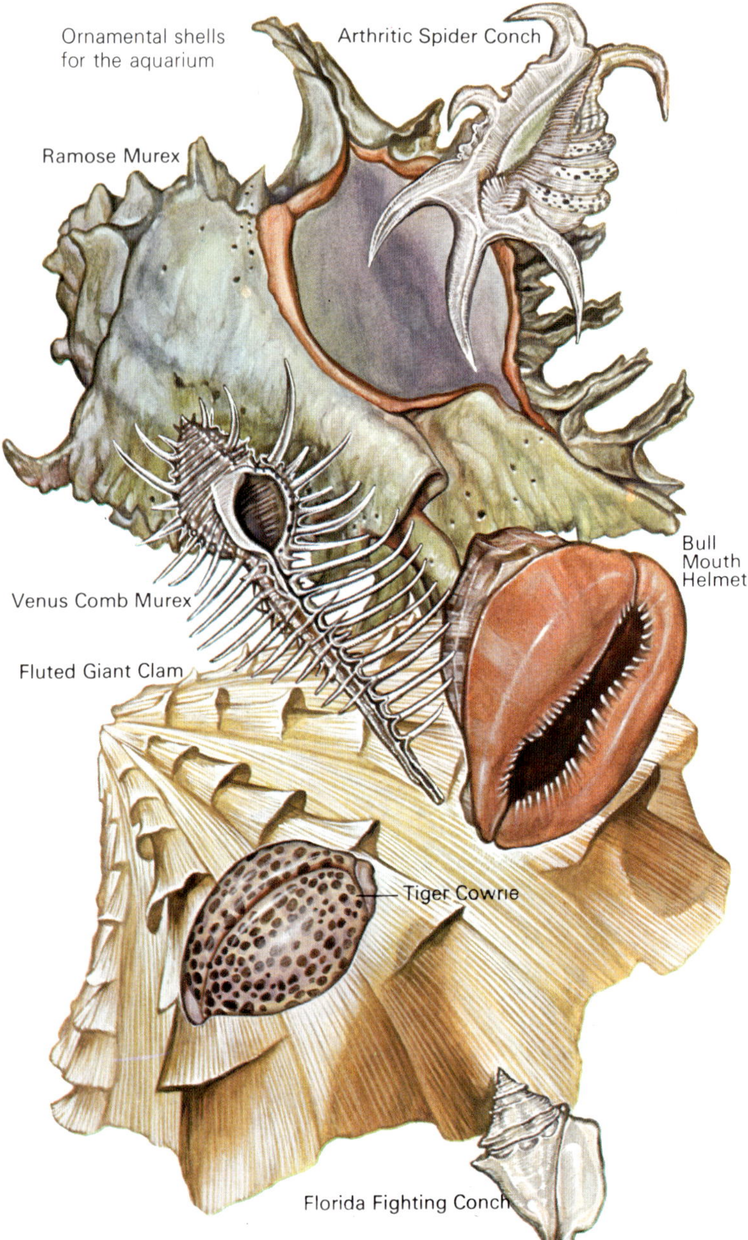
Ornamental shells for the aquarium
Arthritic Spider Conch
Ramose Murex
Bull Mouth Helmet
Venus Comb Murex
Fluted Giant Clam
Tiger Cowrie
Florida Fighting Conch

various animals such as other molluscs, crustaceans, fishes like the triggerfishes, reptiles, birds or mammals (including man), and the resistant, inorganic shell is slowly worn away as it rolls over the sea bed.

The vast majority of shells used to decorate the marine aquarium are those of the univalve molluscs. Examples of the more common of these are the conus, cowrie, murex, cameo shells, batswings, spiders, scorpions and conches.

Certain shells of bivalve molluscs, i.e., molluscs which secrete a shell in two more or less distinct halves, are also used in the marine aquarium. The giant clams and the scallops are examples, but these are not nearly so intricate and attractive as shells of the univalves and consequently are not so popular.

The sea shell in the marine aquarium has three functions:–

(i) **Decoration** The vast majority of tropical sea shells are large, colourful and beautiful in form and are therefore of aesthetic value as decor items in the aquarium. Many of the new-comers to the hobby of marine aquarium keeping became interested via another very absorbing hobby – Conchology, the study and collection of sea shells.

(ii) **Refuge** By imaginative placing within the aquarium almost all sea shells can be used to provide an intricate network of galleries and passages which are used continually by nervous and shy fishes as 'hideouts' and night-time resting places.

(iii) ***p*****H buffering** The calcium and magnesium salts making up the shells are almost entirely the carbonate salts, and as such are invaluable aids for maintaining the water *p*H at the correct alkalinity.

A sea shell as sold by a dealer is rarely fit to be placed straight into the sea aquarium. All too often some part of the dead animal is trapped inside the shell and this would quickly foul the water if placed in the tank. To avoid this possibility, all shells should be treated by steeping in a bleach solution for three days, washed under a running tap for one hour and finally boiled in a stainless steel or enamelled saucepan for two hours, prior to positioning in the tank.

Corals

Many marine aquarists experienced in culturing delicate invertebrate organisms, maintain several heads of live coral in their sea aquaria. The less experienced aquarist uses dead corals for aquarium decor, provision of refuges and for the *p*H buffering effect which these items produce as a bonus.

The vast coral reefs of the world have been built up painfully slowly over hundreds of years by tiny colonial animals whose close relatives are the much larger anemones. The dead coral underlying today's living reef was formed hundreds of thousands of years ago, and if one were to drill deep enough, coral stone would be reached which was formed hundreds of millions of years ago by the remote ancestors of the present-day coral polyps.

Coral polyps also have the ability to extract certain salts, mostly calcium carbonate, from sea water. They secrete these salts from surface cells, building up a stone-hard tube around themselves protecting them from predators and if growing near the high-water mark on a shallow sloping reef, from desiccation during the short period they are exposed to the tropical sun. These polyps are mostly colonial and neighbouring tubes fuse together to produce the relatively large structures we recognize as coral heads of various species.

When selecting pieces of coral to enhance the sea aquarium, it is better to 'shop' for pieces of the right size and shape to fill a pre-selected space, rather than buying coral on impulse and then attempting to force it into arbitrary places in the tank.

Generally speaking, the following hints may help regarding the positioning of the coral. Pieces of coral of the same species should be grouped together, and tall pieces kept to the rear of the tank. Try to build up to a high spot towards the rear of the tank which is well off-centre, and introduce colour in the tank decor by using organ pipe coral (*Tubipora*). This is the only coral in which the calcareous skeleton itself is brightly coloured. It is a vivid scarlet colour and is always a welcome feature in any sea aquarium decor.

No matter how clean a piece of coral appears to be when purchased, it should always be cured in the manner given for treating shells. It is important that no smell of chlorine should persist on the coral when it is placed in the aquarium.

Rock and corals suitable for aquarium decor. 1 Finger Coral, 2 Lettuce Brain Coral, 3 Branch or Elkhorn Coral, 4 Rose Coral, 5 *Fungia* Coral and 6 Brain Coral.

FISHES FOR THE AQUARIUM

Spotted Ray (*Dasyatis kuhlii*)

The rays, like the sharks, belong to a class of fishes known as the elasmobranchs. The elasmobranch fishes are all characterized by the possession of a cartilaginous rather than a bony skeleton. The lack of a rigid superstructure means that the location of the internal organs is not as secure as in the bony fishes of the class Actinopterygii, and so great care must be taken when handling them out of water. In my opinion, many small sharks and rays which refuse to feed

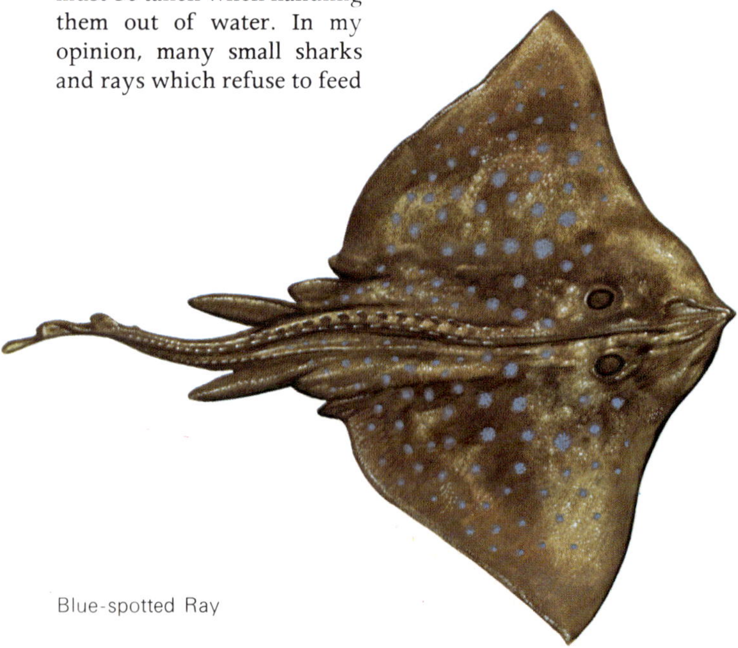

Blue-spotted Ray

Nurse Shark

in captivity do so because the viscera have been seriously dislocated by clumsy handling before the animals were sold to the collector.

The feeding of a Spotted Ray in good condition in a large tank presents few problems, as the fish shows a marked preference for crustacean and molluscan flesh. It is unlikely that these fishes will ever accept dried foods, showing interest only in fresh protein.

Nurse Shark (*Ginglymostoma cirratum*)

One of the few sharks suitable for culture in the marine home tank, the Nurse Shark is often available in smaller sizes down to about 13 to 15 in (33 to 38 cm). It is impossible to obtain this species any smaller than this because the female is *ovoviviparous*. This means that although there is no placental development of the embryo as in mammals, the female is fertilized internally and the embryo develops within her body, until at birth, the infant emerges as a fully formed dwarf version of the parents. This species can grow to around 14 ft (4 m) in length, but seldom exceeds 20 in (51 cm) in a 6 ft (2 m), 120 gallon (540 litre) aquarium. Although the Nurse Shark is reputed not to be a man eater, there are several well-authenticated accounts of serious attacks on young bathers in the Caribbean, usually caused by teasing of the adult sharks.

The Nurse Shark, being *demersal* or bottom-dwelling in habit, is one of the few members of the shark family that can breathe when stationary. The *pelagic* sharks which move freely at all depths in the ocean are, with a few exceptions, unable to breathe unless continually on the move.

Feeding Nurse Sharks in the sea aquarium presents few problems because they are scavengers and therefore have small appetites once tank acclimatized. Difficulties in starting them to feed can usually be overcome by offering squid, mussel or prawn flesh in the evening, when they become more than usually active. They appear to rely almost entirely on the sense of smell to enable them to detect food. The sympathetic shark owner will bear this in mind in the early attempts at feeding, taking into account any currents in his tank when deciding where to drop the foodstuffs, so that the scent of the food is carried to the shark.

Soldierfishes (*Holocentrus* spp)

The soldierfishes or squirrelfishes are primarily nocturnal fishes. This is indicated by their large eyes and, perhaps less obviously, by their bright red basic coloration. Most nocturnal reef fishes are predominantly red in colour. A soldierfish is a voracious predator and must never be trusted in community with fishes small enough to be accommodated in the capacious mouth. However, once a specimen is well adjusted to aquarium life, it will learn to accept chunks of flesh provided that it can see the food falling through the water. Few members of this genus will take static food particles from the floor of the aquarium, no matter how hungry they are.

Soldierfish

Sea-horses and pipefishes (Family Syngnathidae)

Sea-horses are often the first marine animals that the novice marine aquarist chooses for his tank. These fishes are undoubtedly of equestrian appearance, caused by the horse-like

Giant Sea-horse

form of the head and their deportment. The latter characteristic is produced because the normal posture of the body is in the vertical plane and the head held at right angles.

Throughout recorded history these unlikely looking animals have excited the curiosity of all who have seen them. Sea-horses have featured on coins, on the signet-ring of a Roman Emperor and on the coats-of-arms of individuals and civic bodies. They feature in the collections of fishes of almost every marine aquarist – until their several disadvantages become apparent. Prime among these were (i.e. until the introduction of gamma-ray irradiated *Mysis* shrimps, their refusal to eat anything except living *Artemia* shrimps. However, aquarists are advised against purchasing these animals, unless:
a) their dealer maintains stocks of frozen gamma-ray irradiated *Mysis* shrimps, as this is the only non-living food which all sea-horses readily accept, and b) a sea aquarium is available whose only other occupants are invertebrates *or* other equally slow fishes, e.g. pipefish, dragonet, etc.

Related pipefishes from the South Pacific are certainly more active and entertaining to observe in a natural system marine aquarium than seahorses, but again they are essentially macroplankton feeders with the same demanding food requirements.

Some specimens of the Banded Pipefish will often show a greater degree of adaptability under aquarium conditions than others. For example, if three pipefishes from the same area are imported from the same dealer, it is quite likely that one or even two will learn to eat gamma-ray sterilized *Mysis*, whereas the third one might starve to death unless the post-importation 'disinclination-to-feed' syndrome is broken.

Caution living sea foods should only be used in systems where medications such as 'cuprazin' (protozoan infections), 'myxazin' (general disinfectant and bacteriocide) or 'sterazin' (fluke and worm infestations) may be used if needed to treat the disease outbreak which will usually follow. Coralfishes have little or no resistance to North Atlantic pathogens.

In order to conserve these food supplies within the

Banded Pipefish

aquarium, particularly during the winter months when such food is not so readily available, it is advisable not to include any other animals within the aquarium which would compete for the food. Juvenile butterfly fishes and angelfishes in particular but, in fact most other small coral fishes, relish small crustaceans and newly born livebearer fry.

Shrimpfishes (*Aeoliscus* and *Centriscus* spp)

Shrimpfishes are related to the sea-horses and like them are characterized by a strong exoskeleton of horny material. A much more striking feature is the curious habit of swimming permanently upside down. Furthermore, the extraordinary mobility and incessant activity of the expressive eyes, coupled with the permanently head-down swimming position, makes the fishes look as if they are forever searching for some treasured possession recently lost. Again it must be said that unless a well-matured natural system tank and thousands of brine shrimp nauplii are available daily, these enchanting creatures should never be removed from their reef homes.

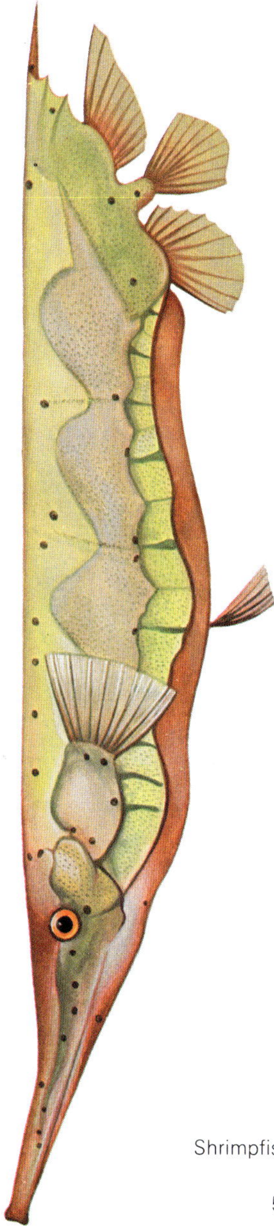

Shrimpfish

Targetfish

Scat

Malayan Angel

Brackish water fishes

Targetfish (*Therapon jarbua*)

These fishes, which are also known as Tigerfishes or Crescent Perches, are equally at home in pure salt water or brackish water, and although they may be maintained successfully in fresh water they seldom appear to be fully at ease. They are probably the hardiest of all fishes that can be kept in a sea aquarium, feeding with great exuberance on all foods. They can become rather boisterous and may subdue the more delicate true reef fishes such as the butterfly fishes so that they hide and slowly starve to death. They are almost disease free, very long-lived and grow rapidly. They are usually low-priced and so are an excellent first choice for the novice aquarist. They are not brilliantly coloured but because they frequently school, a dozen or so in a large tank is an impressive sight.

Scat (*Scatophagus argus*)

This fish's systematic name translates into English most unfortunately as the 'Hundred-eyed Muck-eater'. This name was acquired because the first specimens examined by western ichthyologists were found to have stomachs full of excrement. Such unsavoury feeding habits, however, are certainly not characteristic of this species if it is provided with more attractive fare. In the sea aquarium, Scats do not prove so hardy as the previous or next species, but they have nevertheless been kept for more than four years by relative beginners in the field.

Malayan Angel (*Monodactylus argenteus*)

In the sea aquarium, Malayan Angels (or Diamond fishes or Moonfishes) should be kept in small groups of three or more because on the reef they occur in dense shoals of up to a thousand fishes, moving with uncanny precision. They tend to be bullied in the aquarium unless provided with adequate retreats. Their low price, readiness to accept even the most mundane foodstuffs and strong resistance to diseases makes them an ideal choice for the beginner. Their close relatives from the West African seaboard, *Monodactylus sebae*, are more attractive but not quite so hardy in captivity.

Six-striped Grouper

Since these three species of fishes are occasionally sold by dealers from brackish and even freshwater tanks, the specific gravity of the water in which they are bought should be carefully checked. If the specific gravity differs greatly from that in the marine aquarist's tank, this imbalance should be slowly corrected by gradually adding tank water to the polythene bag in which the fishes were carried home.

Groupers (Family Serranidae)

The next six fishes to be described are strongly recommended to the more ambitious beginner. They are all very hardy, quite colourful, will eat almost any form of fresh protein and are not particularly susceptible to diseases.

In the wild state, the grouper or rock cod lives a very leisurely life, punctuated at intervals by sudden powerful lunges from its rocky lairs with mouth agape to engulf an imprudent passer-by. In the sea aquarium, however, this characteristic behaviour may be significantly modified. The relatively high intelligence, good memory and excellent eyesight shared by members of the grouper family means that they soon come to recognize their owner and commence the unusual behaviour of swimming up and down in the open as soon as he enters the room.

Six-striped Grouper (*Grammistes sexlineatus*)

The Six-striped Grouper is a very intelligent fish and at its juvenile size of about 1½ to 2½ in (4 to 6 cm), it is safe with almost any other fishes. However, in common with other fishes of its family, it has an exceedingly large mouth, a

Jewel-spotted Grouper

characteristic which, as the fish grows larger, may be the beginning of the end for the smaller damselfishes, clownfishes, etc., which share its home.

Jewel-spotted Grouper (*Cephalopholis argus*)

The wide range of this species has given rise to some variation in colouring, but broadly speaking the reddish-brown background colour scattered with bright blue circles, is typical of the species. Like all the groupers, it swims slowly by alternate movements of the pectoral fins using only the powerful back muscles to thresh the tail fin when the forward-lunge mechanism is triggered. In this respect the feeding habits of the groupers are very similar to those of the fresh-water pike. In captivity, the grouper quickly realizes that continued taking of small live fishes for food is a hungry policy, and after a few days it is quite ready to receive small chunks of any kind of flesh.

Cephalopholis boenacki

As with other groupers, this species soon learns to accept any kind of flesh such as squid, cockle, lancefish, etc. This species in particular is hostile to other fishes of this genus and even other fishes of this species. Even a male and female will be mutually hostile if placed together out of the breeding season and so it is preferable to keep them individually rather than in pairs. Many marine fishes, and the groupers are no exception, have the ability speedily to change their coloration to match a particular shade in the environment or simply to display an

Cephalopholis boenacki

emotion. An indication of the hardiness of this fish is its tremendously successful ability to colonize the tropical oceans of the world.

Cephalopholis boenacki has been reported from places as far apart as East Africa and Singapore. As with other large groupers, feeding presents no problem. When the fish has once settled into its new home, it should be given a day or so before food is offered. The new owner should be sympathetic enough to realize that capture, air freight and introduction to aquarium life is a disturbing experience for most fishes. For a highly territorial animal like the grouper which derives its psychological security from total familiarity with a small area, this sudden removal into an entirely different habitat may border on the traumatic.

Epinepholus flavocaeruleus

This is perhaps the most gorgeous of all the groupers. The coloration of this fish both in range and tone of colour is almost identical to the totally unrelated Powder-blue Surgeonfish (*Acanthurus leucosternon*, see page 92). It is interesting to speculate why two fishes of enormously different habitat should have similar coloration. The grouper is a territorial lurking animal which is fond of caves and highly predatory, and the surgeonfish is an open water, shoalling fish, feeding on algae and macroplankton. Whatever the reason, the lucky owner of this grouper must surely rejoice at the generosity of

Epinepholus flavocaeruleus

nature in producing two fishes of such exquisite coloration.

As with other groupers, new fishes to the aquarium should be allowed two or three days to familiarise themselves with their new environment before feeding is attempted. After this time their fear of their owner and the new territory will have been overcome by the pangs of hunger and, on offering sizeable chunks of fresh protein, the owner will be rewarded by the usual grouper-lunge as the fish spots the descending piece of meat and, with unbelievable speed, rushes from its lair. The groupers may be kept in community with other coral fishes, provided that all the other fishes are at least as large as the grouper and preferably larger.

Pantherfish (*Chromileptis altivelis*)

The Pantherfish is not brilliantly coloured but is nonetheless characterized by a most striking pattern of blue-black circular spots on a rich greyish brown background. A striking feature of this fish is the ludicrously small proportion of the head in relation to the remainder of the body. The chromatic tints of turquoise, gold and silver refracted by the fins are of indescribable beauty when the fish is caught at the right angle and the eyes radiate emerald-green malevolence like those of a pagan idol. However, this baleful expression is counterbalanced by the most comical paddling of the absurdly large pectoral fins, and so the total impression on the observer is an amusing rather than fearful one. The

Pantherfish

Pantherfish will nevertheless quickly eat any animal small enough to fit its enormous mouth.

When fishes of this species come to know their owner, they spend less of their time indulging in the classical grouper activity of lurking and may become quite bold, swimming almost continuously in the open spaces between corals and rocks. With its outlandishly large fins fully spread, a good-sized Pantherfish is an impressive sight when swimming prominently in the aquarium.

Cerise Grouper (*Variola louti*)

This grouper is a rare and treasured beauty in British aquarists' tanks for it is hardly ever imported into Great Britain. It is not rare in the wild but collectors experience extreme difficulty in extracting it from its lair and at the same time retaining all their fingers intact.

This fish's control of body colour is highly developed, perhaps more than any other grouper. When at rest, it is a most uninspiring russet-brown colour with the slightest hint of blue spots liberally scattered on the body. If a small live fish is introduced into the tank, a miraculous change in appearance occurs. Almost imperceptibly and then with gathering momentum, the fish's whole body becomes suffused with an indescribable shade of red. Small islets of sapphire blue radiate a strange glow as the fish's body pulsates with light a few seconds before the 'grouper-lunge'. On the completion of this act the colours subside and until the next meal time, peace reigns in the tank.

Cerise Grouper

Wreckfish (*left*) and Royal Gramma (*bottom*)

Wreckfish (*Anthias squamipinnis*)

This fish belongs to the family Anthiidae. It is available in two distinct forms which occupy the same territory on the same reef and so there may well be sexual variation within the same species. To date my collector has been unable to confirm this theory, since he has not witnessed any spawning activity in the species.

This fish has a manner of swimming reminiscent of *Amphiprion* species to which, of course, it is not even distantly related. The whole body undulates with a slow sinewy grace as the large pectoral fins alternately paddle back and forth with seemingly little effect. A beginner not acquainted with this species could be forgiven for thinking that the fish was distressed owing to its unusual mode of progress through the water.

Feeding a newly imported Wreckfish can be nerve-racking because they are frequently reluctant to begin taking dead foods in captivity. The first Wreckfish I ever caught came from a small reef off Mozambique. Although it survived the arduous 2,000 mile (3,200 kilometre) road journey from the East African coast to Central Africa, once home it refused all food, even baby guppies, for nearly two weeks. One morning it accepted a guppy and, from then onwards, its progress to full acclimatization proceeded without event. After ten days on live guppies followed by three days on freshly killed baby guppies, it accepted its first feed of dead protein. This was a small morsel of fresh steak impaled on the end of a toothpick. The feeding of *Anthias* spp. has, however, become less of a problem since the author's introduction of sterilized *Mysis* shrimps.

Royal Gramma (*Gramma loreto*)

This beautifully coloured fish of the family Grammidae was once believed to exist only in relatively deep water, below about 30 to 40 ft (9 to 12 m) in the Caribbean area. However, due to the efforts of various collectors in the area, it has been found that the Royal Gramma exists in quite shallow water, 3 to 6 ft (1 to 2 m), but it is very difficult to detect owing to its habit of swimming upside down in caves and under ledges. It is as if the fish feels that its abdominal region is particularly vulnerable, and it seldom swims with the ventral surface of its body more than a few millimetres away from a solid surface. It is carnivorous and in the wild probably feeds on various macroplankton, i.e., small crustaceans, larval and juvenile fishes, etc. Comments regarding feeding are the same as for the previous species.

Cardinal fishes (Family Apogonidae)

Cardinal fishes (*Apogon* spp) are quite hardy fishes and can be recommended to the beginner as excellent species with which to commence marine fish keeping, apart from the fact that they rarely accept dried food in captivity. Most species have to be fed small live fishes, or after a period in captivity, fresh protein such as minute pieces of earthworm, prawn and steak, etc. These species are mouth-breeders, that is to say that the fertilized eggs are retained in the parent's mouth for incubation, and so it is possible that cardinal fishes may be among the first species of marine fishes to be successfully bred in captivity.

The movement of cardinal fishes is strange in that it takes the form of short spates of slow forward motion followed by long periods of total inactivity. During this time, the dainty little creatures appear to be suspended in mid-water in a slightly head-down attitude, as if hung by invisible threads.

Goatfishes (Family Mullidae)

The goatfishes of the genus *Pseudupeneus* rank with the Striped Catfish (*Plotosus anguillaris*) and the Spotted Ray (*Dasyatis kuhlii*), as the few bottom scavengers suitable for the average-sized marine tank. However, the goatfishes are not noted for their beauty of form, though both the red and yellow species are very strikingly coloured. As befits most scavenging organisms, they have a very wide taste in food-stuffs. Food that no other self-respecting coral fish would swim anywhere near is frequently snapped up from the bottom with a relish not easily disguised. However, this readiness of the fishes to dispose of surplus food must not be an excuse for laxness in tank management. Decaying organic matter lying around on the aquarium floor will not benefit in the long run either the goatfishes or any other occupants of the tank.

Cardinalfish (*top*) and Goatfish (*above*)

The batfishes *Platax pinnatus* (above), *P. orbicularis* (above right) and *P. teira* (right)

Batfishes (Family Platacidae)

The batfishes commonly available to the marine aquarist at the time of writing are illustrated opposite. They present something of an enigma to the aquarist owing to their curious inclination for flying into a panic at the slightest provocation when in unfamiliar surroundings. Once acclimatized, however, they have few equals; they have undemanding tastes, extreme resistance to all diseases, a high rate of growth and aquarium longevity. This applies wholly to *Platax orbicularis*, slightly less so to *Platax teira*, and slightly less still to the beautiful *Platax pinnatus*. *P. orbicularis* may even be regarded as a beginner's fish for those lucky enough to afford to begin their hobby with large tanks, but *P. teira* is best not purchased until one has at least six months experience, whereas *P. pinnatus* should not be purchased by anyone unless they can afford to house two, three or more of these beautiful creatures on their own in an 80 gallon (360 litre) or larger aquarium.

The batfish *P. orbicularis* will take any kind of fresh protein and at various times I have owned adaptable individuals who, when really hungry, would even take dried food. Specimens of *P. teira* will, however, only accept fresh meat such as prawn, *Mysis*, etc., whilst *P. pinnatus* usually commences feeding on small live earthworms or *live Mysis*.

The batfishes soon learn to detect the vibrations and, later, the visual stimuli of the owner's approach to the aquarium. Even before the cover is raised, the hungry fishes will often cavort at the surface of the water in eager anticipation of the titbits to come.

For fishes which grow so large – specimens up to 12 in (30 cm) in depth are not uncommon – batfishes appear quite defenceless and are badly at the mercy of the aquarium's 'bullies'. Most fishes lacking either sharp teeth and/or sharp spines show high speed retreat as a defence system. The batfishes, however, seem to have been curiously neglected in the evolution of these defensive measures and, whereas the young fishes will often drift motionless in a current, closely resembling dead leaves or pieces of seaweed, the adults have none of this guile and must presumably rely on some objectionable substance in their skin or mucus secretion to deter predators.

Angelfishes (Family Pomacanthidae)

Koran Angelfish (*Pomacanthus semicirculatus*)

This species of angelfish is found more frequently than any other in home marine aquaria. It is a very successful species, ranging from East Africa across the Indo-Pacific to Ceylon and into the Pacific Ocean to the Philippines. Unlike many other marine fishes with a wide range, there is surprisingly little variability in colour and form within the species. It is almost impossible to differentiate between a specimen from Kenya and one from the Philippines. However, although little variation is seen among adult fishes, the variation in colour pattern among developing juveniles within this genus is amazing. Below are shown some phases in the development. This phenomenon has created a great deal of confusion in the ranks of amateur taxonomists. Animals of the same species but at different stages of development have been named as new species, and even attributed to different families.

Once acclimatized to the aquarium, which rarely takes more than two to three days, the Koran Angelfish is an excellent

Colour variation in juvenile and adult forms of the Koran Angelfish

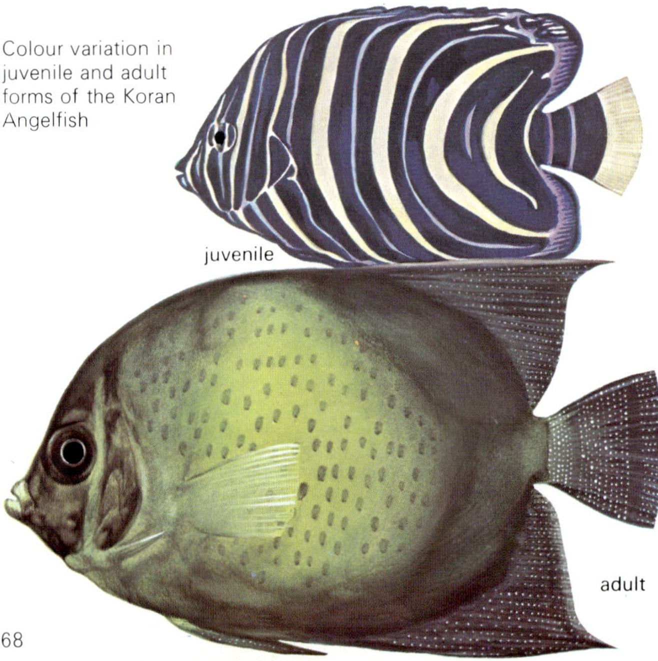

aquarium fish accepting all foods with rewarding eagerness. Unfortunately it is somewhat prone to White spot disease, but this protozoan infection is easily cleared with appropriate medication, i.e. Cuprazin (no invertebrates) or Myxazin.

Emperor Angelfish (*Pomacanthus imperator*)

The adult of this species is one of the most spectacular marine fishes. When familiar with its surroundings, the Emperor or Imperial Angelfish moves effortlessly around the sea aquarium with a sense of majesty and circumstance which prompted early German marine aquarists to bestow the name 'Kaiserfische' on the species.

The Emperor Angelfish is a little more demanding than the previous species with regard to water quality and even the slightest trace of nitrite in the water seems to quickly debilitate the animal, making it prone to diseases which it would otherwise resist. *Benedenia* is a commonly seen infection among newly imported specimens, or those kept in less than perfect sea water. This is easily cured if the animal is

Juvenile and adult appearance of the Bluering Angelfish

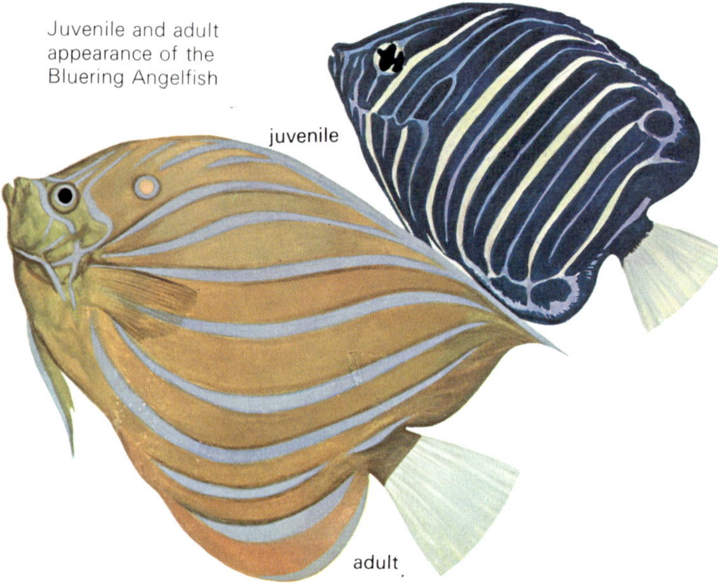

promptly transferred to exceptionally clean water and treated with Cuprazin or sodium sulphamezathine – dosage: one teaspoonful of solution to 10 gallons (45 litres) of water. If the latter treatment is used, the fish should be transferred to fresh sea water five days after the disappearance of symptoms, to avoid massive kidney damage which may otherwise result. Live foods may be necessary to tempt the Emperor Angelfish to begin feeding in captivity, but it will soon move on to various forms of fresh protein.

Bluering Angelfish (*Pomacanthus annularis*)

The similarity between juvenile forms of this fish and the preceding two species can be a source of great confusion to the beginner, as the illustrations show. All three fishes have a juvenile patterning of white lines on a radiant blue background. The following points may help the beginner to be certain of which species he is buying in the absence of expert advice from a dealer. In the Koran Angelfish the white stripes are slightly curved or shaped, but they are much more curved

Juvenile and adult forms of the Purple Moon Angelfish are similar in appearance.

with one near the tail forming a completely closed ellipse in the Emperor Angelfish. In the Bluering Angelfish the white stripes are almost straight, only the ends curving inward slightly towards the tail.

Foods offered initially to the Bluering Angelfish will probably be live foods, for example freshly sterilized mussel cut into shreds, chopped earthworm, whiteworm and live brine shrimps. The healthy Bluering Angelfish will, however, quickly graduate to more convenient forms of frozen foods

Purple Moon Angelfish (*Pomacanthus maculosus*)

Although not so spectacularly coloured as the previous species, the adult specimen of *P. maculosus* has beautiful elongated tips to the posterior edges of the dorsal and anal fins and is a most graceful swimmer. It is perhaps the most hardy of all the larger angelfishes, having a high resistance to disease and a very adaptable appetite. Furthermore it is one of the cheapest of the angelfishes and can be strongly recommended to the beginner after he has gained initial experience with damselfishes and clownfishes.

Feeding presents no difficulties whatsoever and although

fishes are initially very shy, after seven to ten days in the aquarium they will continually display their pleasing colours at the front of the tank. All foods are eagerly accepted. The very similar angelfish *P. asfur,* from the same small area of the North Kenya coast up to the Red Sea, is easily distinguished from *P. maculosus* by having a bright yellow tail.

Black or Grey Angelfish (*Pomacanthus arcuatus*)

This species and the very similar French Angelfish below are restricted to the Caribbean area and in common with other sea aquarium fishes from this area, appear to be more than usually prone to *Lymphocystis* disease. This may be because, in my experience, American shippers of coral fishes tend to house all fishes of the same species together. That is to say that a large shipper will have one tank full of Rock Beauties, another full of Queen Angels, and so on. This inevitably results in a certain amount of intraspecific aggression and in consequence many epidemal cells become ruptured, thus permitting the ingress of *Lymphocystis* viruses which are responsible for the characteristic creamy to pinkish-white cysts.

When juvenile, both the Black Angelfish and the French Angelfish are extremely similar, both being black with four vertical bars down the sides. However, the stripes of the Black Angelfish are white, whereas those on the French Angelfish are yellow. When adult, *P. arcuatus* becomes a pewter grey colour with black dots on every scale. In a good specimen filaments extend on the dorsal and anal fins almost to the posterior edge of the caudal fin.

French Angelfish (*Pomacanthus paru*)

The adult of this species is considerably smaller at 12 to 15 in (30 to 38 cm) than the Black Angelfish at 18 to 22 in (45 to 55 cm). As previously stated, the vertical barring on the juvenile is a daffodil yellow colour, making it a much more attractive fish. It is also considerably more attractive as an adult, characterized by a charcoal grey to blackish body colour with the posterior margin of each scale having a creamy white to pale yellow edge. If anything, the French Angelfish is a little more fussy than the Black Angelfish with regard to feeding, although both species do well once settled into a suitably

Juvenile (*top left*) and adult (*above*) Black Angelfish with juvenile (*top right*) and young adult (*below*) French Angelfish

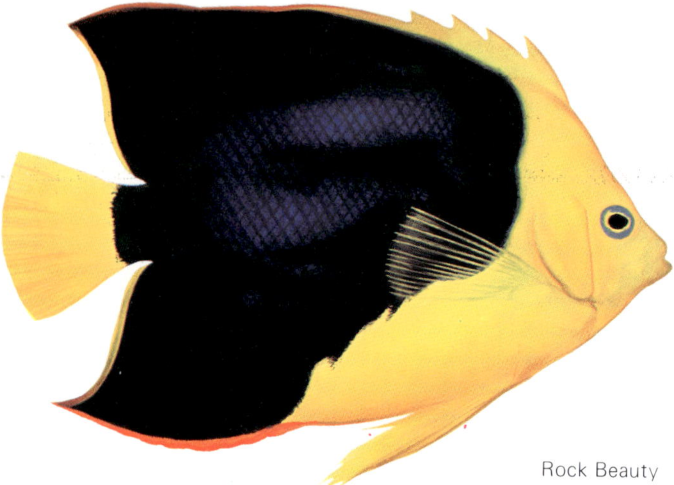

Rock Beauty

designed habitat. Adequate cover must be provided.

One cannot overstress the need for complete peace and quiet for a fish newly introduced into a sea aquarium. All too often, I am the recipient of agitated telephone calls from beginners asking why, despite the fact that they have offered ten different foods in the space of as many minutes, their newly purchased butterfly fish or angelfish is still cowering behind a rock. Nothing can be relied on more to send a nervous coral fish into a state of deep shock than this sort of behaviour.

Rock Beauty (*Holocanthus tricolor*)

This splendid fish adorned in yellow, black and orange red with a sapphire blue eye, is one of the toughest angelfishes from the Caribbean. I have kept several specimens of this slow growing species for well over four years. Once adjusted to home aquarium life, they greedily accept all forms of food, and like the surgeons and tangs and other marine angelfishes, particularly relish the frequent inclusion of fresh spinach and chopped lettuce in their diet. This is very important to remember for the aquarist maintaining a tank under the clinical system. The algae growing naturally on the corals and rocks of the natural and semi-natural system tanks will probably provide adequate green stuff without other additions.

Queen Angelfish (*right*) and the colour variation Blue Angelfish (*left*)

Queen Angelfish (*Holocanthus isabelita*)

There are two distinct colour variations of the Queen Angelfish, which have been called the Blue Angelfish *(H. ciliaris)* and Townsend's Angelfish (*H. townsendi*), although taxonomists tend to recognize only one species. The Queen Angelfish is a breathtakingly beautiful animal and again, limited only to the Caribbean area. Smaller specimens between 2 and 5 in (5 and 12 cm) do well in the home aquarist's 25 to 80 gallon (112 to 360 litre) tanks although to grow one of these creatures to its full size of 12 to 18 in (30 to 45 cm), several years of care in a 150 to 200 gallon (675 to 900 litre) home aquarium would be needed. Like all the angelfishes, the Queen Angelfish has a characteristic razor-sharp curved spine on the base of each operculum (gill cover), and in the aquarium two fishes of the same sex (or of different species) will raise their spines and wound each other with vicious slashing movements, if they feel that their territory is being threatened. In the wild it is probable that real fights only result from the most severe provocation, but the aquarist must realize that his tank is not a full-sized coral reef and offers few places for the vanquished to retreat to safety. Generally speaking one should never place two angelfishes together unless:–

(i) they are at widely different stages of development as shown by their colour patterns;

(ii) the two fishes had been collected as a mated pair, or

(iii) they are of different species.

Even if these conditions are met the union should only be attempted if an adequately sized reserve tank is available.

Chequered Angelfish (*Holocanthus xanthurus*)

This angelfish, like the Purple Moon Angelfish, is also strongly recommended for the recent beginner who wishes to try his hand at something a little more demanding than damselfishes. This angelfish comes mostly from the reefs around Ceylon, and will often commence feeding in the aquarium within twenty-four hours of its introduction.

As with almost all the more delicate reef fishes, that is the butterfly fishes, surgeons, tangs, sweetlips, wrasses, etc., the angelfishes do not feel at all happy if placed into 100 per cent fresh synthetic sea water. For this reason, it is much better to place them in an aquarium which has previously contained less demanding fishes for a month or so. This means that the water has had time to mature and that the gravel overlying the filter plate will contain a significant population of nitrifying bacteria, ensuring that both excreted ammonia and nitrites are rapidly and safely metabolized to harmless nitrates. If this is done, the newly introduced coral fishes will never have to tolerate a dangerous concentration of toxic ammonia and nitrites. The exceptions to this rule are of course the Caribbean angelfishes previously referred to. Because of their susceptibility to *Lymphocystis* viruses, it would be better to place them in a solution of one of the pre-aged synthetic salt formulae such as 'Natura' sea salt.

Majestic Angelfish (*Euxiphipops nevarchus*)

This glorious fish exhausts all superlatives. In prime condition it puts even the Emperor Angelfish to shame. Found on most of the reefs surrounding the Philippines group, it is only

Chequered Angelfish (*above*) and Majestic Angelfish (*below*)

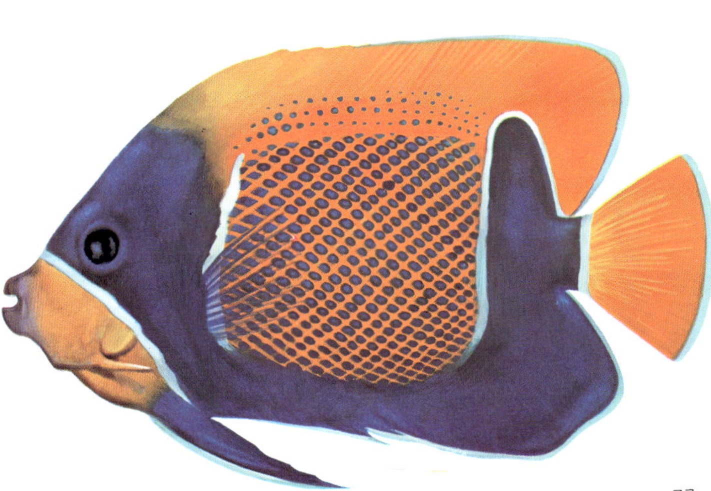

available in Great Britain for a considerable sum and large specimens are of course much more expensive. Large public aquaria lucky enough to have a Majestic Angelfish on exhibition usually proudly display the fact in the entrance.

This is one of the more difficult marine fishes to persuade to start feeding in captivity and one must certainly provide either well-matured sea water in 'good-heart' or a pre-aged preparation. However, even these precautions are not necessarily guarantors of success with this species.

Purple Fireball Angelfish (*Centropyge fisheri*)

Although having only two colours, deep purple and fiery orange, this small fish, adult at 2 to 2½ in (5 to 6 cm), is the cherished ward of many competent aquarists who maintain only a 20 to 30 gallon (90 to 135 litre) tank. It is a shy and secretive little creature, even after it has learnt to associate its owner with food and security. A properly furnished aquarium for this species will take this fact into account and adequate provision for caves, rocky shelters and spatial coral intricacies should be made. This species may be restricted in range to the coral reefs of East Africa.

Coral Beauty Angelfish (*Centropyge bispinosus*)

This pretty little angelfish extends over a wide area of the tropical shallow waters from East Africa to the Philippines and beyond. Its beauty is not as immediately striking as that of *Centropyge fisheri,* but it is nevertheless attractive. Both the Coral Beauty and the Purple Fireball will peacefully co-exist in the same sea aquarium provided that adequate territory is provided for each of them.

Centropyge argus

This attractive angelfish is not often seen and is believed to be quite rare throughout its range in the Caribbean, where it is rarely found at depths less than 100 feet (30 metres). This species and the previous two fishes are sometimes known as dwarf angelfishes.

Coral Beauty Angelfish (*top*), Purple Fireball Angelfish (*centre*) and *Centropyge argus* (*bottom*)

Butterfly fishes (Family Chaetodontidae)

Yellow Longnose Butterfly fish (*Forcipiger longirostris*)

This fish has quite unjustifiably been labelled an 'impossible' by several writers, some of whom appear to have never even attempted to keep it. The impression that this fish is difficult to keep is undoubtedly conveyed by the enormous lengthening of the upper and lower jaw. This is an adaptation to facilitate the removal of small molluscs and crustaceans, etc. from within coral heads and would suggest that the fish is a finicky feeder. However, this fish is so tough and adaptable in captivity that it will accept all manner of the usual aquarium foods within a few days of introduction to a tank. The Yellow Longnose is at least as tough and hardy as another much maligned butterfly fish, *Chelmon rostratus*, but it takes to aquarium feeding much more readily than this species.

A fish of this species in good condition illustrates why the common name for the family is butterfly fishes. Most people have watched or collected butterflies when young and are familiar with the insects' resting stance with both wings touching and in the vertical plane. The butterfly fishes are all strongly compressed laterally, and consequently in shape and often in markings, they resemble butterflies in the resting position. The slightly spasmodic movements of these fishes when searching for food among rocks and corals is also not

Yellow Longnose Butterfly fish

unlike the fluttering of butterflies.

The Yellow Longnose Butterfly fish is strongly recommended to anyone who feels that he has the confidence, and preferably the experience, to tackle this family which includes some of the truly 'impossibles', for example *Chaetodon trifasciatus*. This impressive butterfly fish is the despair of even the most experienced and competent aquarists because of its refusal to eat anything other than the polyps of living corals.

Copper Band Butterfly fish (*Chelmon rostratus*)

Apart from the obvious differences in coloration, etc., this fish strongly resembles in shape the previous species, although the jaws are slightly less elongated in relation to the body size.

The Copper Band Butterfly fish may be difficult to encourage to start feeding in captivity. This is particularly true of those specimens originating from the Singapore area rather than those imported from the Philippines. However, provided that conditions in the aquarium are excellent with regard to correct physical (lighting, specific gravity, temperature, etc.), chemical (*p*H, low toxin content, etc.) and psychological (adequate cover, absence of aggressors, etc.) parameters, this lovely fish will nearly always be tempted with slivers of fresh mussel mantle or squid. From then on, it will feed readily.

Copper Band Butterfly fish

Wimplefish

Wimplefish (*Heniochus acuminatus*)

This butterfly fish is very unlike the other members of the family, with lengthened rays of the dorsal fin and a generally high body. It is strikingly adorned with black stripes on a silver background. Wimplefishes seldom present any difficulties with regard to feeding. They readily accept all foods, including dried flake offerings and freeze-dried products.

Although there are several species within this genus, for example *H. permutatus, H. singularis, H. cornutus*, the Wimplefish is the commonest, cheapest, hardiest and, in my opinion, the prettiest member of the genus. An extremely successful reef fish, it is widespread in distribution from the reefs of tropical East Africa, through to the far eastern atolls of the Central Pacific and shows remarkably little variation throughout its range.

When juvenile, like some other members of the family

Chaetodontidae, Wimplefishes will often be seen swimming up to other much larger fishes, and starting to peck away at their flanks, heads, fins and gills. It is presumed that these juveniles are fulfilling the same function as the Cleaner Wrasse (*Labroides dimidiatus*) in ridding the larger fishes of troublesome ectoparasites. As a result of a certain similarity in external appearances, the Wimplefish is sometimes mistaken for the Moorish Idol (*Zanclus cornutus*), although the two fishes are not at all closely related.

Golden Butterfly fish (*Chaetodon auriga*)

Regarding its numerical superiority, this fish is probably the most successful within its genus. Its range is identical to that of the Wimplefish, but the sheer weight of numbers in the areas in which it is found indicate that it is a remarkable colonizer. It is sometimes known as the Threadfin Butterfly fish. In view of its ubiquity, one might expect the connoisseur of marine animals to be uninterested in it. However, it is popular even with marine aquarists of long standing.

Although a common and hardy butterfly fish, this species is by no means the hardiest in captivity. That honour falls to the Sunburst Butterfly fish – the ideal butterfly fish for the beginner.

Golden Butterfly fish

Black-wedge Butterfly fish (*Chaetodon falcula*)

This butterfly fish also has a wide range from the Indo-Pacific through to the Central Pacific, but it is not numerous anywhere. It is also known as the Saddled Butterfly fish. It is certainly not among the easiest butterfly fishes to keep with regard to starting it feeding in the aquarium. However, like the Copper Band, once feeding has begun in earnest, the Black-wedge Butterfly fish proves to be one of the most indestructible of all the sea aquarium occupants.

Unlike *C. auriga, C. lunula* and *C. kleini,* this butterfly fish is seldom obtainable in small sizes. Most specimens seen offered for sale are young adults around 3 to 4 in (7 to 10 cm) body length. This may well account for the difficulties often experienced in getting the Black-wedge to feed in captivity. It is not unlikely that an adult fish would have already formed very definite feeding habits and preferences for certain items of diet not available in the sea aquarium. Modifying such established habits might prove more difficult for an older fish than for a relatively young one.

Moon Butterfly fish (*Chaetodon lunula*)

After the Sunburst Butterfly fish, this fish is possibly the next most trouble-free member of its genus. After several months study of the special requirements of the most difficult family of coral fishes to successfully culture in the home sea aquarium, the novice may feel competent enough to try his new found skills on *C. lunula* and *C. kleini*. The Moon Butterfly fish has the same wide range as *C. auriga* and *C. falcula*.

In the sea aquarium, the Moon Butterfly fish soon settles down and apparently loses all fear of its owner. The body colour is unusual among coral fishes and unique among butterfly fishes in that it is predominantly a dark olive-green.

Butterfly fishes are not especially aggressive towards other coral fishes except members of the same sex and species, although in an overcrowded tank some threat display may be seen. This almost always takes the form of head-down circling movements with all fins extended. The needle-sharp points of the dorsal fin rays are stiffly erected, and short forward thrusting movements generally suffice to deter transgressors from any further antagonism.

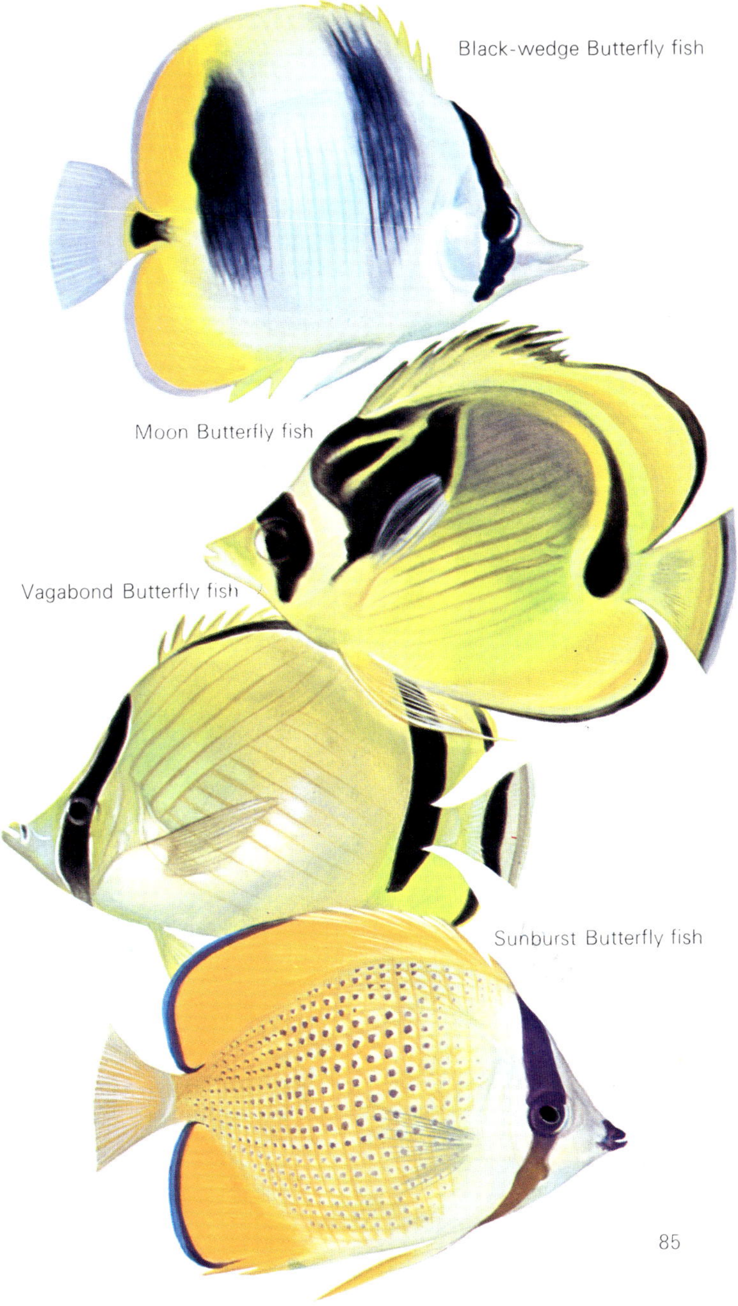
Black-wedge Butterfly fish
Moon Butterfly fish
Vagabond Butterfly fish
Sunburst Butterfly fish

Vagabond Butterfly fish (*Chaetodon vagabundus*)

This fish, which is also known as the Criss Cross Butterfly fish, and the very similar *C. pictus*, do not do particularly well in the home aquarium, although, as with all rules, there will always be notable exceptions. The main reason for illustrating the fish here is to warn all except very experienced aquarists from including this fish in their collection. The principal problem which is experienced is its refusal to feed adequately and consistently in the sea aquarium. In consequence, the nutrients it gleans from its finicky picking among the corals, rocks and gravel, hardly seem to supply the requirements of its *basal metabolism* (the basic minimum chemical activity of an organism necessary for the maintenance of the life processes). *Mysis* is usually the first food accepted.

Sunburst Butterfly fish (*Chaetodon kleini*)

The flanks of this fish have an attractive golden coloration, each scale being picked out with a darkish spot. These spots under normal top lighting appear to be blue-black, but when the fish is seen under reflected front light, it will be noticed that both the spots and the vertical head stripes are a rich purple-blue colour.

This fish is unique among the family Chaetodontidae for its hardiness, resistance to disease and eagerness to feed in captivity. It is sometimes known as the White-spotted Butterfly fish. Of the butterfly fishes, this species is probably the easiest to keep.

Brown Butterfly fish (*Chaetodon collare*)

Almost all fishes of this species offered for sale come from the reefs and shallow waters surrounding India, Pakistan and Ceylon. The beginner has already been advised not to purchase specimens of this species. A small proportion of those fishes I have cultured have not responded to even the most painstaking efforts, unless *Mysis*/*Artemia* were available.

The Brown Butterfly fish is included here because its coloration, an unusual purple-brown, is rare among coral fishes, and also because it is a rather difficult subject, it will constitute the sort of challenge that the advanced marine aquarist may care to take up one day.

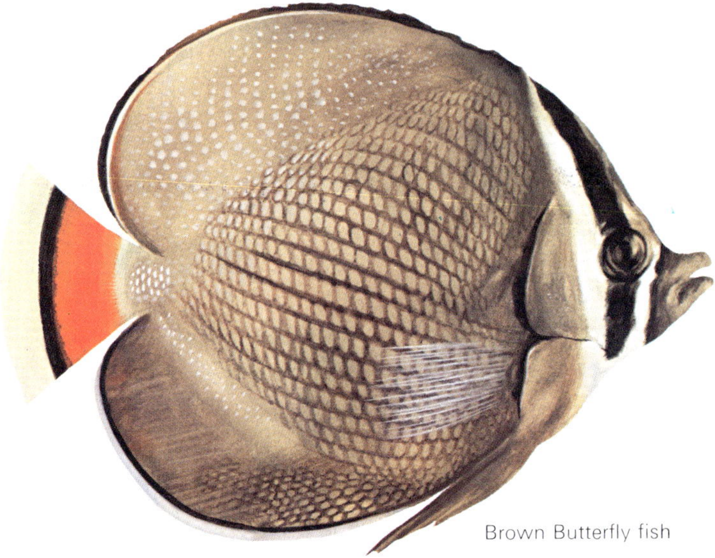

Brown Butterfly fish

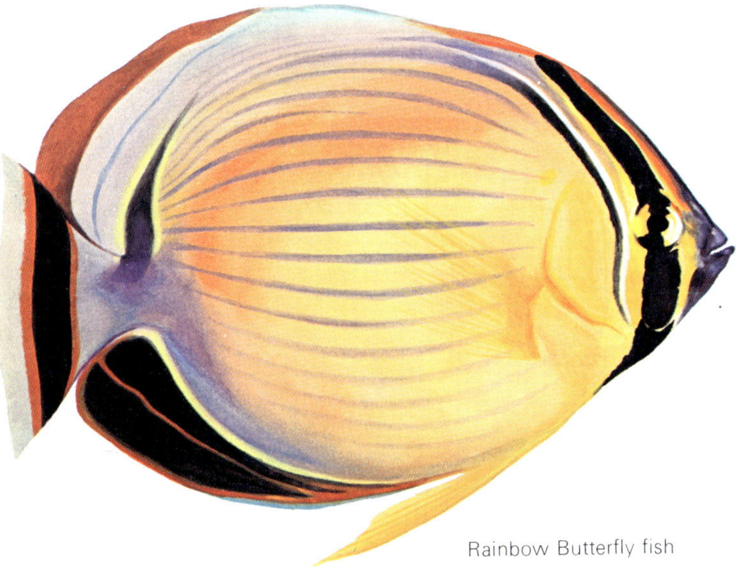

Rainbow Butterfly fish

Rainbow Butterfly fish (*Chaetodon trifasciatus*)

This species, also known as the Lineated Butterfly fish, is probably the most beautiful fish in the whole genus. Unfortunately, however, it is also the most exasperating for it frequently refuses all normal foods offered to it in captivity. The following notes may be of use to aquarists attempting to keep this difficult fish for the first time.

Firstly, a large specimen should be obtained, between 3 and 4 in (7 and 10 cm) which is extremely fat. A butterfly fish of any species which is 'narrow' behind the head should never be bought. Secondly, a large, approximately 80 gallon (360 litre) aquarium should be used with pre-aged synthetic sea water and a great deal of rockwork and coral formations. Feeding should start with live coral heads, followed by half-grown brine shrimp larvae and, after a few weeks, the fishes should be weaned on to vitamin-soaked freeze-dried brine shrimps or *Mysis*.

Addis Butterfly fish (*Chaetodon semilarvatus*)

This richly coloured species comes only from the Red Sea, and its distinctive coloration and markings make it easy to spot in films made by Captain Jacques Cousteau in that area. A specimen in prime condition will always show the several orange-yellow bars on the flanks and the purple-grey eye spot.

If this butterfly fish is kept at the normal temperature of 75 to 80°F (24 to 26°C), its basal metabolism appears to proceed at a very slow rate. This is probably due to the fact that this species comes from the lukewarm waters of the Red Sea and has therefore evolved a body chemistry capable of withstanding the losses due to high saline content and high temperature of the water. I had one exceptionally recalcitrant specimen which for a time refused all foods. During this period there was no noticeable decline in activity or reduction in weight. One day it suddenly accepted prawn eggs and has never stopped feeding greedily since. It is now almost two years old in captivity but was clearly adult at 5 in (12 cm) when imported.

The significance of this experience, which has often since been repeated with this species, is that any other butterfly fish with its high basal metabolic rate, would have wasted

Addis Butterfly fish

Four-eyed Butterfly fish

away without food in fifteen to twenty days. Individuals in captivity show considerable variation in habits and needs. One specimen may accept every food offered, including dried foods, whereas another will refuse all but small pieces of fresh protein. With all butterfly fishes it will be found that regular (twice weekly) feeds with a properly formulated vitamin complex such as 'SeAvita' will be of invaluable assistance in keeping the fish in as good as, or occasionally in better, condition than when it lived on the reef. On the reef it was subject to predation by groupers, sharks, barracudas, moray eels and had to compete with many other reef animals for the available foods. Probably the easiest way of adding such a vitamin preparation to a food is to dissolve the crystalline vitamin mixture in a little tap water and then soak freeze-dried pieces of brine shrimp in the solution for twenty-four hours in the refrigerator. The resulting food must be kept in the refrigerator at all times since, once added to water and allowed to attain room temperature, many of the vitamins are prone to swift oxidation.

Four-eyed Butterfly fish (*Chaetodon capistratus*)

This fish is found only in the Caribbean area. Although it has often been reported to be hardy in captivity, it does not compare in this respect with the Sunburst Butterfly fish. The black spot and the disruptive dark bar through the eye probably cause predators to confuse the back end for the front.

General hints for the care of butterfly fishes

(1) These coral fishes are very prone to shock if mis-handled at any time during their transfer to the home aquarium. The styrofoam-lined box in which the fishes are transferred home *must not* be suddenly opened in a brilliantly lit room. If it is daytime the curtains should be drawn. If in the evening, the room lights should be extinguished with the exception of a low-wattage table lamp. Needless to say, the aquarium lights should be off, and should be left off until the following day.
(2) Established fishes in the aquarium should be well fed prior to the introduction of the new fishes.
(3) Butterfly fishes should never be placed in sea water with even a trace of nitrite or ammonia contamination. If this

advice is ignored, it is certain that even if the narcotic effect of these toxins is not immediately fatal, the general weakening effect they will have on the fishes will so lower their natural resistance to disease that they will quickly succumb to a multiple infection and die.

(4) Butterfly fishes smaller than 2 in (5 cm) should never be purchased. Infant fishes this size need to feed on planktonic life-forms and coral polyps almost continually for twelve hours per day. Unless the aquarist has unlimited time, patience and brine shrimp hatching facilities, it is unlikely that he will be successful in raising young fishes.

(5) When choosing a butterfly fish from a dealer's tank, always look for the following characteristics:–

(i) The fish should possess the light coloration typical for the species. Any darker than normal fishes should be viewed with suspicion.

(ii) The respiratory rate, indicated by the frequency of the gill cover movements, should be around 80 to 100 movements per minute, assuming that the water temperature is normal at 75 to 80°F (24 to 26°C), and that aeration and filtration are adequate.

(iii) A healthy fish will not swim with the pelvic fins permanently clamped to its belly, but will from time to time lower them and swim for several seconds with them extended. (This is also a guide for indicating the state of health of the closely related angelfishes).

(iv) If possible, always try to witness the butterfly fish feeding on foods you can procure before making a purchase.

(v) A fish which is active and displays an inquisitive interest in its environment is usually a sounder fish than one which is shy and retiring.

(vi) No matter what the state of health of the fish, do not buy either *C. trifasciatus* or *C. pictus*. Fishes of these species together with *C. larvatus* and *C. octofasciatus*, are best left to the very wealthy and/or skilful, and certainly should never be bought by beginners.

One final tip can be given for butterfly fishes reluctant to feed. Few can resist a juicy live coral head and although such a delicacy is expensive, it is sometimes worth while to persuade an expensive fish to feed.

Surgeonfishes and tangs (Family Acanthuridae)

Emperor Tang (*Acanthurus chrysurus*)

All the fishes in the surgeon and tang family are so called because of the existence of razor-sharp 'scalpels' tucked into hollow sheaths at the base of the tail. When angry or afraid the fish can raise these devices at right angles to the body and, as a result of a threshing action of the tail, inflict terrible wounds on the body or fins of an adversary. These fishes will not hesitate to inflict the same sort of treatment on a human hand, so the greatest possible care must be exercised if handling a member of this group.

Like all the members of this family, Emperor Tangs have a great liking for green-stuff in their diet. Three or four times each week, these fishes should receive a good feeding of freshly thawed frozen spinach, or better still, fresh spinach. Such vegetation does not, of course, exist in the fishes' natural environment, and so most coral fishes have to be taught to eat it. This is best achieved by allowing the fishes to fast for a whole day. Then, on the first feed of the following day, spinach (or even chopped lettuce) should be offered. Usually the fishes will be so hungry that they will swallow the proffered food without realizing what they have eaten, and an increasingly strong liking is usually developed for this valuable food. All the surgeonfishes and tangs are swift and powerful swimmers, and have a real need for large open spaces within the aquarium.

Yellow-green Striped Surgeonfish (*Acanthurus lineatus*)

This fish ranks with another member of its genus, *A. bleekeri*, as one of the most pleasingly shaped and graceful movers on the reef. Its range is circum-tropical in shallow seas and on reefs, but it is absent from the tropical Atlantic. This surgeonfish is a most undemanding species to feed, and will readily take all the usual aquarium foods.

Powder-blue Surgeonfish (*Acanthurus leucosternon*)

The novice aquarist is advised not to attempt to keep this species until he has had several months' experience with less difficult members of the genus.

Powder-blue Surgeonfishes do not have a wide range and

Emperor Tang

Yellow-green Striped Surgeonfish

Powder-blue Surgeonfish

Majestic Surgeonfish

are most common in the Indo-Pacific. The species travels rather badly and, when selecting a specimen, greater than normal care should be taken to insure that the fish is completely unmarked. In addition, the areas around the head and chest should be an enamel white colour and any fish which is a dirty grey or off-white colour in this region should be studiously ignored. The dorsal fin of a healthy Powder-blue Surgeonfish will usually be slightly erected; a fin clamped to the body indicates disease and a stiffly erected fin shows that the fish has recently been badly shocked.

The abnormal length of the intestine of this species indicates that it is primarily herbivorous in the wild. In the sea aquarium, however, a healthy specimen will soon learn to eat live foods and even fresh protein. Vitamin-soaked brine shrimp is an excellent 'starter' for the species.

Majestic Surgeonfish (*Acanthurus bleekeri*)

This species is restricted in its distribution to the Red Sea area, where it is never common, and so it is a fairly expensive fish to buy. It is sometimes known as the Striped Surgeonfish. It is not only one of the most graceful and beautifully coloured of the coral fishes, but it is also undoubtedly one of the most undemanding. Its advantages are weakened only by the fact that many specimens become increasingly intolerant of certain other species as they reach the three- to four-year-old stage. A three-year-old Majestic Surgeonfish I own has recently dispatched an adult batfish (*Platax teira*) and an adult *Pomacanthus annularis*. Both of the attacked fishes were large and powerful and had lived with the surgeonfish for the previous two years. The fishes were killed during the night and were found the following morning covered in wounds from the sharp 'scalpels' of the surgeonfish.

Regal Tang (*Paracanthurus hepatus*)

The Regal Tang has been described as 'the bluest thing on earth'. This tang is ideally suited to the smaller sea aquarium, since it becomes adult at about 4 in (10 cm). It is probably a schooling fish on the Philippino reefs where most specimens come from, and so does not object to the company of members of its own species. Even a small sea aquarium of 36 × 18 × 18

Regal Tang

Japanese Tang

in (90 × 45 × 45 cm), i.e., 40 gallons (180 litres), can safely house two or three specimens at $1\frac{1}{2}$ to 2 in (4 to 5 cm).

After its introduction to the aquarium, the Regal Tang or Flagtail Surgeonfish, usually goes into a state of mild shock and will frequently terrify its new owner by lying flat on the gravel under a stone or coral head, or leaning against the side of the tank. However, provided that the over-anxious aquarist can desist from prodding and poking the frightened fish, and assuming of course that the water is in good condition without even a trace of nitrite content, the hardy little fellow will always rally round.

Japanese Tang (*Naso lituratus*)

I have not been able to discover whether this colourful species is very common in Japanese waters, but it is not common anywhere throughout the remainder of its range in the Indo- and Central Pacific.

The 'scalpel' device of the surgeons in this tang is modified to form two bony extensions which are permanently erected in the mature fish. As a result of this feature, any attempts to move this species from one tank to another should always be made using a special type of net made by sewing a polythene bag on to a normal net frame, and then cutting holes in the bag for drainage. If a nylon or cotton net is used, the opercular spines will become entangled in the net and serious damage to the fish will result.

The Japanese Tang has a real need for considerable amounts of vegetable matter in its diet, although like most marine herbivores it soon acquires omnivorous habits.

Sailfin Tang (*Zebrasoma veliferum*)

Remarkable variation occurs in coloration of this species over its range. Indo-Pacific specimens have a complicated coloration, whereas those from the Central Pacific (the East Indies) have the simpler black and white alternate barring. The Indo-Pacific race is generally tougher than the race from the Central Pacific, although the latter is quite hardy and specimens will live for well over seven years if purchased as young 2 or 3 in (5 or 7 cm) fishes.

Large specimens of this species become very active in the

early evening, a period which in the wild probably coincides with the heaviest feed of the day. It would thus be cruel to house a Sailfin Tang, or any other semi-pelagic species, in an aquarium which was not at least twelve times longer and three times wider than the overall length of the fish. This means that a good-sized specimen should be housed in a tank at least 6 ft (2 m) long and 18 in (45 cm) wide and between 18 to 24 in (45 to 60 cm) in depth. Smaller specimens of some 2 to 3 in (5 to 7 cm) overall could be housed in the popular sized 36 × 12 × 15 in (90 × 30 × 38 cm) sea aquarium, where they would probably remain dwarfed throughout their lives. The mechanism by which the ultimate size of a fish is closely related to the size of the aquarium in which it is housed is imperfectly understood, and should form the subject of a serious study. One theory is that when the concentration of some of the fish's waste products reaches a certain level, these products begin to act as growth inhibitors. This may well be partly correct since the growth of certain fishes (in particular *Pterois* spp) will recommence as a result of regular fresh water changes.

Sailfin Tang
Central Pacific form

Moorish Idols (Family Zanclidae)

Moorish Idol (*Zanclus cornutus*)

The Moorish Idol is paradoxically probably the most photographed but least understood coral fish kept in the sea aquarium. Its bizarre shape and striking coloration have always attracted the attention of the artist and photographer and it is consequently the tropical marine fish best known to the general public. It has an extensive Indo-Pacific range, being found off Zanzibar and Maurituis and throughout the Indian Ocean to the Central Pacific.

Although it seems to have a superficial resemblance to the Wimplefish, it is difficult to imagine two fishes which are more different. Whereas the Wimplefish will eat almost any foods offered, the Moorish Idol frequently drives its owner to distraction by refusing even the most tasty titbits. The Wimplefish usually remains free of disease in captivity whereas the Moorish Idol will fall victim to every pathogenic bacterium, protozoan and virus it comes across.

An aquarist of my acquaintance, determined to be the first to succeed with this difficult species, heard from a merchant sailor that he had seen large shoals of Moorish Idols feeding unperturbably on ships' waste in the waters of a Filipino dockyard. Reasoning that the missing ingredient for this species was good, old fashioned filth, he placed two ounces of raw steak into his aquarium and left it to rot. Thirty-six hours later, he had not only killed his Moorish Idol but had prematurely terminated the lives of six other previously healthy and happy fishes. If the aquarist had paused to consider the problem, he would have realized that even if the sailor's doubtful story had been accurate, the fishes, which were presumably driven into the harbour waters by the lack of a certain food on the reef, could simply turn round and swim back out to the gin-clear waters of the reef as soon as they had had enough of the filthy harbour water – not a facility available to the aquarist's fishes. With regard to the authenticity of the sailor's story, I once watched a group of eighteen to twenty adult Moorish Idols every afternoon for nearly a month in the Indian Ocean. They refused to swim any nearer than 200 yds (180 m) to where a stream used as an open sewer by a native village, emptied into the sea.

Rabbitfish

Moorish Idol

Rabbitfishes (Family Siganidae)

Rabbitfish (*Lo vulpinus*)

This close relative of the Moorish Idol is sometimes called the Badgerfish because of the patterning in black and white around the head. It never seems to have enjoyed great popularity. The species has a rather limited range in the Pacific Ocean but is common around the Philippines. Although a shy species, it feeds exceptionally well in captivity. It is odd in that at eight to ten day intervals it sheds its mucous body coat and secretes another one.

Snappers (Family Lutianidae)

Arabian Snapper (*Lutianus kasmira*)

Only two species of this genus have been included here but this is not because these fishes are especially difficult to keep. On the contrary, in common with damselfishes, any of the snappers may be confidently recommended to the complete beginner.

The Arabian Snapper or Blue-banded Sea Perch, is often obtainable at juvenile sizes of 1½ to 2½ in (4 to 6 cm). At these sizes it is quite manageable, but a most gluttonous feeder. If the aquarist could spare the time, feeding these fishes on the

Arabian Snapper

hour every hour would be quite acceptable to them. When they smell the presence of food in the water or optimistically observe the approach of their keeper, a wild form of behaviour similar to that of a shark 'frenzy' invariably results. Should the aquarium house several of these fishes, the surface of the water appears to 'boil' with their greedy, mad threshings.

As these fishes become increasingly boisterous with growth, it would be wise to house them only with fishes of phlegmatic constitutions such as triggerfishes, lionfishes (*Pterois* spp and others) and groupers.

Emperor Snapper (*Lutianus sebae*)

This is a most distinctive species both in coloration, markings and body shape. The Emperor or Red Snapper is characterized by the same gross feeding habits as the preceding member of the genus, but very quickly grows to a much larger size. Exceptional specimens up to 30 in (76 cm) in length are occasionally taken by anglers off East Africa. It is not common

Emperor Snapper

anywhere but the species does have a wide range throughout the Pacific and Indian Oceans. Only the juveniles, which are usually sooty black and white, are found in shallow reef waters, the adults usually moving in groups over deeper water.

An unusual feature of this fish is that, as it grows older, the darker bars lighten from black, through dark brown to reddish-brown, and at maturity the fish is a rich mahogany red colour. When excited, a flush of salmon pink colour spreads into the white areas.

Grunts and sweetlips (Family Plectorhynchidae)

Polka-dot Grunt (*Plectorhynchus chaetodonoides*)

Until the introduction of sterilized *Mysis*, this attractive and non-aggressive species was shunned by most collectors. The reason for the Polka-dot Grunt's bad reputation among marine aquarists was simply that it would only rarely feed well in captivity with the then-available foods. Happily, the ready availability of *Mysis* shrimps has changed that, and this

Polka-dot Grunt

creature is increasingly found in the collections of aquarists able to offer it a quiet tank with no boisterous occupants.

The major problem with the Polka-dot Grunt, as with all other contemporary 'impossible' marine fishes is that of getting the fish to feed substantially in the sea aquarium. The fishes need to derive enough energy from food, not only to replace that expended in maintaining the basal metabolic processes (i.e. digestion, respiration, osmo-regulation etc.), but also to maintain sufficient reserves to repair damage to the body, and, if the animal is juvenile, to promote further growth. It is not enough for the fish to pick here and there in a desultory fashion.

The range of this grunt is from Malaysia to the most eastern coral islands of the eastern Pacific.

Striped Sweetlips (*Gaterin lineatus*)

Although this attractive fish is related to the previous species, it is exceptionally hardy and eager to feed in captivity. In larger tanks it may quickly reach a size in excess of that which the owner originally expected. Thirty inch (76 cm) specimens may be occasionally seen in public aquaria.

Demoiselle or Damselfishes (Family Pomacentridae)

Green Forktail Damselfish (*Chromis cyanae*)

It has been mentioned more than once so far that the damselfishes are ideal species for the beginner. Unfortunately, however, it is inadvisable to include more than one member of each species in an aquarium less than 60 gallons (270 litres) capacity, unless one has been lucky enough to obtain a definite male and female pair.

The Green Forktail Damselfish (sometimes called the Blue Chromis) is the exception to the rule and like the common Mediterranean Brown Forktail (*Chromis chromis*), it is naturally a schooling fish. This means that even in a small 30 gallon (135 litre) sea aquarium, half a dozen or so of these iridescent blue-green beauties may be kept together without too much fighting.

On the reef, a large school of fifty or so adults will face into a prevailing current and periodically dart forwards to

Striped Sweetlips

Green Forktail Damselfish

capture some planktonic morsel of food. In the home aquarium these pretty fishes quickly settle down to a varied and undemanding diet of dried food, chopped earthworm, prawn flesh, chopped heart or steak and whiteworm, etc.

Sergeant Major (*Abudefduf saxatalis*)

The Sergeant Major has a truly circum-tropical distribution, being almost as common on the reefs of the tropical Atlantic as it is in the Pacific, Indo-Pacific and Red Sea, where it lives in small communities. The amazing hardiness of this fish has to be experienced to be believed. On my last collecting trip to the Indian Ocean before returning to England, I brought back to Zambia a collection of reef fishes which included two Sergeant Majors. When the time came to dispose of equipment and animals among fellow aquarists, the marine fishes could not be placed owing to the then current lack of marine experience and interest among aquarists. A Dutch friend finally agreed to accept them but I later learnt that, quickly tiring of their aggressive behaviour and lack of bright colours, he had disposed of them by dropping them into a brine shrimp hatching tank, containing only cooking salt solution – and nine months later they were still alive and thriving.

Sergeant Major

Humbug Damselfish

Humbug Damselfish (*Dascyllus aruanus*)

The Humbug Damselfish is one of the most aggressive members of a family noted for aggression. Its sense of territory ownership is well developed and makes life particularly difficult for the importer, who, because of the popularity of the species as an inexpensive, attractive beginner's fish, must always carry large stocks. In a large tank, however, between 60 and 80 gallons (270 and 360 litres) or larger, a small 'family' of six to eight of these fishes will quickly settle in, each one taking up station in its allotted territory which it only really leaves to chase off an intruder or to snap up food. Apart from their alertness and smart appearance, hardiness, low cost and aesthetic value in complementing the more obvious impact made by larger fishes, Humbug Damselfishes have a definite ecological niche to fill in the sea aquarium. At meal times they definitely reduce the dangers of organic pollution of the sea water by catching scraps of food which would otherwise go entirely unnoticed by the bigger fishes. They will survive dangerously high nitrite levels, eat anything remotely edible, tolerate temperatures from 70 to 85°F (21 to 30°C) and with the minimum of effort on the part of the aquarist, go from strength to strength in unsatisfactory artificial seawater formulae. As such they are most invaluable to the impecunious beginner since, forgiving the mistakes he will probably make, they will survive all. The Humbug Damselfish is found in all shallow seas in the tropics except the tropical Atlantic.

Cloudy Damselfish (*Dascyllus carneus*)

This is an exceptionally pretty fish whose colours are very much understated. The Cloudy Damselfish is found from East Africa to Ceylon, although it is only in the latter waters that it is as common as the Domino Damselfish.

Domino Damselfish (*Dascyllus trimaculatus*)

When juvenile or newly imported, this species, which is also sometimes called the Three-spotted Damselfish, is a deep sooty black all over with little or no trace of iridescence. As it matures in captivity, the intensity of the blackness may decline somewhat so that it becomes a dark, metallic grey colour. It may well be, however, that this change is due to some deficiency in captivity since 3 to 4 in (7 to 10 cm) specimens can be seen on the reef which are still showing total

Cloudy Damselfish

melanism though obviously adult. Recent work has shown that a diet rich in vitamins of the D group will correct this loss of colour.

The Domino Damselfish is strongly territory defending in behaviour, and will often show its displeasure at the violation of its spatial possessions by rapidly oscillating up and down in the water, somewhat resembling a yo-yo on an invisible string. It has other ways of expressing anger and resentment. The marine aquarist may be suddenly aware of a deep throaty porcine grunting noise in a lounge or fish-den whose pig population is conspicuously non-existent. Initial feelings of alarm will usually be replaced by amusement on discovering that this surprisingly audible noise issues from the damselfishes in the sea aquarium.

I have witnessed the spawning of Domino Damselfishes once and Cloudy Damselfishes twice in my 80 gallon (360 litre) aquaria. On each occasion, the mode of reproduction was noticeably similar to that of the freshwater family of fishes Cichlidae. An initial courtship display consisting of face to face slow circling, accompanied by much fin quivering

Domino Damselfish

and body shaking, takes from twenty minutes to one-and-a-half hours to complete. Then the female, from whose vent a short, blunt white ovipositor tube protrudes, proceeds to deposit a string of quite large (0·75 mm in diameter) fawn-coloured eggs on a stone, shell or coral surface. Having completed a row of five to twelve eggs, she retires and the male, who has meanwhile been defending the spawning site from all intruders, now moves in and sprays the eggs with milt. This procedure is repeated until the female is exhausted of eggs. The eggs were left with the parents but the fry were unfortunately eaten either by the parent fishes or by other fishes in the tank.

Black Velvet Damselfish (*Abudefduf oxydon*)

It is difficult to believe that this gorgeous creature is related to the Sergeant Major. It is the most magnificent fish in the damselfish group, and because it is quite rare in the Philippines from where most specimens originate, it is never cheap.

Saffron-blue Damselfish (*Pomacentrus melanochir*)

This species is sometimes also called the Yellow-tailed Damselfish. The colouring of this species is simple, with a radiant blue body and a yellow tail, but the overall effect is most spectacular. Most Saffron-blue Damselfishes in Europe came originally from the reefs around Ceylon where the fish is quite common.

Black Velvet Damselfish

Saffron-blue Damselfish

When buying these fishes for the small home sea aquarium, buy either only one of each species, or, with a larger tank, nine to twelve of each species. If only two are purchased and even if the fishes are a male and female pair, apart from the spawning season when they will just tolerate each other, there will be incessant bickering and fighting between them. Strangely enough, when a relatively large number of the same species are housed in the same tank, very little real aggression occurs, although there will still be occasional threatening behaviour. The probable explanation for this is that, in large numbers, each fish becomes slightly bewildered as to which of its fellow residents it should attack first, and in consequence seldom attacks any of them.

Electric-blue Damselfish (*Pomacentrus caeruleus*)

This species is very common around the Philippine group of islands. It is as aggressive as any other of the damsel family, so when stocking average sized aquaria, the rule will again be one only per tank.

Many of the damselfishes show a marked preference for demolition and excavation work, and perhaps in no other member of the family are these talents more highly developed than in the Electric-blue Damselfish. Many a marine aquarist

Electric-blue Damselfish

with a flair for decor in the arrangement of his corals, rocks, shells and gravel etc., has seen his artistic creation slowly but resolutely redesigned by a small damselfish. However, tolerance is a small price to pay for the pleasure and amusement afforded by such a beautiful creature. As with all damselfishes, anything and everything is eaten with great relish.

Clownfishes (Family Pomacentridae)

Common Clownfish (*Amphiprion percula*)

The Common Clownfish, or Orange Anemone fish, is ever popular because of its availability, good colour, relative hardiness and low cost. It is comparatively low priced by collectors in Singapore and the Philippines and so it is probably a very common and easily caught fish in these areas.

This species is commonplace in public aquaria, dealers' shops and the home aquarium and has probably been as responsible as the Moorish Idol and the sea-horse for many 'converts' to the pleasures of marine keeping. In no other species is the most typical coral fish feature, the sudden division between two adjoining colours, so highly developed.

These fishes are among the most sociable of all coral fishes and many of them may be kept in one aquarium with very little fighting. They like a high temperature, between 78 and 80°F (26 and 27°C) and will thrive on almost any foods available. This latter accommodating tendency should not be abused, however. A meal two or three times weekly of fresh protein (chopped liver, steak, prawn, squid etc.) or even better, live food such as chopped earthworm, will greatly improve their colour and general breeding condition.

It is most fascinating to see these fishes nestling down among the tentacles of a sea anemone. The members of the genus *Amphiprion* have, without exception, evolved a *symbiotic* union with anemones of the *Stoichactis* genus and, ideally, should always be kept with an anemone. (A symbiotic union is a relationship between two organisms in which both parties directly benefit from the arrangement). The thousands of nematocysts (stinging cells) on each tentacle would paralyse and kill the clownfish if they fired. However, the anemone, benefitting as it does from food brought to it by the clownfish, never fires off the nematocysts at the fish after an initial introductory period, and thus protects it from attacks by other fishes. These would be promptly stung to death if they were foolhardy enough to pursue the clownfish into the anemone's deadly embrace.

Common Clownfish

Fire Clownfish (*Amphiprion ephippium*)

The Fire or Tomato Clownfish is found throughout the Central Pacific, from Singapore to the island atolls of the eastern Pacific. Specimens from Singapore may be a dark chocolate-brown colour on the body, whereas most from the Philippines are a glowing orange-red. This fish is rather aggressive towards its own species and only one should be kept per tank, unless one is lucky enough to obtain a mated pair – a bond which incidentally appears to be permanent.

Black Clownfish (*Amphiprion sebae*)

This fish, like the previous, may tolerate others of its species when young, but as it approaches sexual maturity at $1\frac{1}{4}$ to 2 in (3 to 5 cm) it becomes intolerant of all but its mate. It too seems to form a permanent partnership, so that if one can

Fire Clownfish

obtain a mated pair, an interesting aquarium can be created with no other life-forms but a large *Stoichactis* anemone and the two fishes. If fed well on fresh and live protein, the pair will usually spawn. A pair I kept in a 70 gallon (315 litre) aquarium spawned eight times at twenty-day intervals between August and December 1969. The eggs were zealously guarded by both parents during the development period when they were attached to a flat stone. As soon as they hatched, however, invariably at three to five o'clock in the morning, the parents ate them before they could be removed.

Chocolate Clownfish (*Amphiprion xanthurus*)

There is a large group of clownfishes, including *A. xanthurus, A. polymnurus* and *A. bicintus,* which may well prove to be variations of a single species in the same way that all batfishes

Black Clownfish

Chocolate Clownfish

may belong to one species showing major geographic variations in colour and form. The Chocolate Clownfish is fairly common throughout the Indian Ocean and the whole tropical Pacific area. It begins to exhibit aggression to others of the species as it matures.

Teak Clownfish (*Amphiprion melanopus*)

This fish, sometimes called the Dusky Anemone fish, is a dull shade of brownish-fawn and is the least colourful species in the genus. It is only really common in Ceylonese waters. Its low price and hardiness recommend it to the marine aquarist who has gained some initial experience with damselfishes.

Pink Skunk Clownfish (*Amphiprion perideraion*)

The unfortunate common name of this attractive fish refers to the white stripe running along the dorsal median surface and not to its smell. It is most common in the Central Pacific areas, although a very similar species (again possibly only a geographical variation) named the Yellow Skunk Clownfish (*A. akallopsis*), is common in the Indian Ocean.

These clownfishes are rather more shy than other members of the genus; in the wild I have never seen them stray more than 8 to 12 in (20 to 30 cm) from the anemone home base. For this reason, whenever possible skunk clownfishes should be kept in small groups of four to six in tanks containing no other fishes, and with adequate anemone provision to keep all the fishes happy. Whereas other clownfishes may do quite well without anemones in the tank, it would be cruel to keep skunk clownfishes under these conditions.

Maroon Clownfish (*Premnas biaculeatus*)

This species, sometimes called the Spine-cheeked Anemone fish, is the aristocrat of the group both in ultimate size and coloration. Maroon Clownfishes are found in the Philippines area but are nowhere common and are usually the most expensive of the family to purchase. In their curious manner of swimming, body shape, and anemone-loving habits they are similar to fishes of the genus *Amphiprion*. Yet, because of several important differences, the most obvious of which are the two curved knife-like appendages on the sides of the head,

Teak Clownfish

Pink Skunk Clownfish

Maroon Clownfish

Saddleback Clownfish

they have been placed in the separate genus *Premnas*.

Aggression is not only noticeable between unmated members of the same species, but there appears to be a historic vendetta between the Maroon Clownfish and the Fire Clownfish. It is either a reckless or a very skilful aquarist who has one of each co-existing in the same aquarium.

Saddleback Clownfish (*Amphiprion laticlavius*)

Although not spectacularly coloured, this species has the twin virtues of reaching a good size in captivity, up to 6 in (15 cm), and also of being generally quite well mannered. Almost all specimens offered for sale in Europe originate in the Philippines.

Wrasses (Family Labridae)

Cuban Hogfish (*Bodianus pulchellus*) and Spanish Hogfish (*B. rufus*)

On the reef, the Cuban Hogfish, sometimes called the Spotfin Hogfish, and the Spanish Hogfish are usually found only in quite deep waters, i.e., seldom less than 30 ft (9 m) deep. However, it is amazing how quickly they adapt to the shallow depths of the home sea aquarium, settling down to become valued members of any collection. In coloration the Cuban Hogfish is rare among diurnal coral fishes in that it is a glorious pink, with enamel white and daffodil yellow markings.

After several months in captivity, these fishes will eat anything they are offered, including even dried flake foods. For the first two weeks under aquarium conditions, however, it may be necessary to offer food which more closely approaches the wild state diet, for example strips of freshly sterilized mussel and squid flesh, prawn meat and prawn eggs.

In January 1968, whilst returning from a business trip to the United States, I stopped at Cleveland, Ohio, to visit the city's magnificent Public Aquarium. After discussing several problems with the Aquarium Director, he and the aquarium's chief diver drove me to Cleveland Airport to continue the homeward journey. However, whilst visiting a marine dealer on the way, my two colleagues made me a gift of a Cuban Hogfish and a Royal Gramma. The weather at the time was unbelievably cold and, although the fishes were kept at cabin temperature on the trans-Atlantic flight, they suffered considerable exposure during the journey from Heathrow to my home. On arrival, I discovered their water to be at 58°F (14°C). The Royal Gramma was very dead and

Cuban Hogfish

Spanish Hogfish

had clearly been so for hours but the hogfish was still breathing very shallowly, although it was completely immobile. The fish was left in its original transit water to avoid needless additional chemical shock and two hours later when the temperature had risen to 76°F (25°C), light aeration was introduced into its bag. The fish began to move around and half an hour later its water was gradually mixed with aquarium water and the fish released into the tank, where it spent the next year in perfect health.

Green Parrot Wrasse (*Thalassoma lunare*) and Chocolate Rainbow Wrasse (*T. purpureum*)

All the wrasses have a curious mode of swimming. The body is moved very little and the fish apparently propels itself along using the pectoral fins only. In the Green Parrot or Moon Wrasse, this curious gait, which causes the fish to 'hop' through the water, reaches its highest development. Of course, when frightened or if pursuing another fish, the wrasse will bring into action the swift lateral undulating movements of the body, resulting in short bursts of speed which are unequalled by any other coral fish. Thus we have the paradoxical situation of a family of fishes whose movements are normally rather slow and clumsy but which, when required, can produce unparalleled bursts of speed.

Anyone who has ever handled wrasses out of water will know that their mucous coating is exceptionally thick and slimy. In fact the common name of one wrasse from the Caribbean is 'Slippery Dick' – a most apt name for the family as a whole. Therefore, when removing a wrasse from the water, great care must be taken if the fish is not, as a result of its own frightened behaviour, to end up on the floor.

The Green Parrot Wrasse and its close relative the Chocolate Rainbow Wrasse both have undemanding appetites. When new in the aquarium, they may be slightly choosy with regard to diet, but once established and living in harmony with the other inhabitants of the tank, they quickly adapt to all food-stuffs. Most fishes in this group, if given a free choice, will select mostly animal protein such as mussel and scallop flesh, crab, prawn and shrimp meat, and so must be regarded as being essentially carnivorous in the wild state. However, they are so adaptable in captivity that few specimens will refuse a good quality dried food when kept in good conditions.

Both species of the genus *Thalassoma* illustrated have a very wide range extending from the East African coast in the west to the most eastern islands of the Pacific, but are absent from tropical Atlantic waters.

Green Parrot Wrasse

Cleaner Wrasse (*Labroides dimidiatus*)

This species, which is sometimes called the Blue Streak, must not be confused with the Neon Goby (*Elacatinus oceanops*) which fulfills a very similar socio-ecological function in the tropical Atlantic. Throughout its enormous range in the Indo-Pacific, Pacific proper and Red Sea, this little wrasse is a very important fish. It removes parasites from all fishes on the reef. It is an astounding sight to see one of these tiny fishes swimming fearlessly into the mouth and gill-chamber of a 40 pound (18 kilogram) grouper which, if it so wished, could consume fifty or more at one sitting. The huge predator never attempts to eat his benefactor, however, although he may be seen to wince occasionally if the little 'doctor' is clumsy in his surgery. The great dependence that many coral fishes must have on the Cleaner Wrasse was recently demonstrated by a field worker who removed all the Cleaner Wrasses from a small area of the

Chocolate Rainbow Wrasse

Cleaner Wrasse

reef for a short period. The decline in both the variety and number of species in the area was considerable, and the missing population did not return until the Cleaner Wrasses were reinstated.

In the aquarium, the Cleaner Wrasse will ideally find an insufficient number of ectoparasites infecting the other fishes and will usually demonstrate its gastronomic versatility by eating normal aquarium foods. It is more than usually susceptible to changes in water quality, and seems to have very little liking for unmatured synthetic sea water or any synthetic sea waters of poor formulation. Consequently, it is not advisable to introduce the fish into sea water less than one month old and even then there must of course be a complete absence of nitrite. All possible precautions must be taken to prevent any kind of shock developing during and immediately after the introduction of this species to an aquarium.

Birdmouth Wrasse (*Gomphosus coeruleus*)

The Birdmouth Wrasse, sometimes called the Hawaiian Birdfish, ranges from East Africa, up into the Red Sea and across the Pacific Ocean. It is distinguished by its magnificent

Birdmouth Wrasse

coloration of deep cobalt blue, with blue-green fins. Another feature which makes confusion with any other species impossible is the elongation of the mouth into a beak-like structure. This fish is one of the hardiest in the family.

Clown Wrasse (*Coris gaimard*)

This fish has been referred to earlier with reference to the astonishing changes in coloration and patterning that take place as it matures. The species *C. formosa* and *C. africana* of the Indo-Pacific and *C. gaimard* of the Central and eastern Pacific may well all be a single species which shows variation over a large geographical range. The most beautiful Clown Wrasses come from the Philippines. In these fishes the red parts of the body are especially vivid.

If inexpertly handled on introduction to an aquarium, all the wrasses can go into a serious state of shock, with rapid breathing, the animal lying on the bottom, often on its side as though dead. The beginner usually reaches for a stick and prods the hapless animal into activity. This has the reverse of the desired effect and often deepens the shock to a fatal level. The tank lights should be turned off, aeration and filtration turned to maximum, and the tank blackened out by covering

Clown Wrasse

with thick cloth or paper. The aquarium should be left like this for a minimum of twelve hours. At the end of this period, after nightfall and with the room lights off, working perhaps with the aid of an assistant's flashlight, the coverings should be removed from the aquarium. Leaving the curtains of the room open, the fishkeeper should now retire from the room. With the light of dawn the following day, the fish will usually be found eagerly searching for food, totally recovered and none the worse for its experience. The larger *Thalassoma, Coris* and *Gomphosus* species will often react to introduction to an aquarium by diving into the gravel and will not emerge during daylight until assured of their safety in the new surroundings. Once settled in, the Clown Wrasse proves a hardy aquarium fish, eating all it is offered but showing a strong preference for fresh protein.

Twinspot Wrasse (*Coris angulata*)

This gorgeous animal is rarely offered for sale in Europe. However, in certain areas of East African reefs, it is a very common wrasse. It is difficult to collect because when approached to within 6 to 12 in (15 to 30 cm) it plummets straight into the sand.

Twinspot Wrasse

Dragonfishes (Family Scorpaenidae)

Common Dragonfish (*Pterois volitans*)

For the beginner not keen on damselfishes and prepared to pay a little more, the Dragonfish (Lionfish or Turkeyfish) is an excellent alternative. It is very hardy, easy to feed and not aggressive to fishes too large for it to eat.

The Dragonfish on the reef is predatory, living on small fishes, but it will learn to eat suitably sized pieces of flesh in the aquarium. For the first ten days or so, it may be necessary to feed it on small, inexpensive freshwater fishes, such as female guppies, but after two days' starvation, a healthy Dragonfish will always accept a small piece of steak or prawn provided that it sees it falling through the water. The movement is important because the fish's feeding response is triggered off only by moving objects.

Dragonfish owners must be careful to avoid contact with the first eleven spines of the dorsal fin, as these contain a toxic venom. A colleague was unlucky enough to run his hands on to these dorsal spines. Immediately he began to suffer shooting pains in the arm and eventually collapsed to his knees. A strong tourniquet was applied and the local emergency service alerted. Fifteen minutes later the affected area was puffing up and the pain was excruciating, but on arrival at hospital the victim was given injections and was soon making a speedy recovery. I tell the story not to deter anyone from buying one of the several attractive *Pterois* species. These fishes use their venomous spines only as defensive deterrents and never as offensive weapons. However, the dangers of allowing a child to own one will be self-evident. The Common Dragonfish has a circum-tropical range, with the exclusion of the tropical Atlantic area.

Regal Dragonfish (*Pterois radiata*)

This exotic looking creature is just as potentially dangerous as the previous species. All comments regarding the Common Dragonfish apply to this species, the only differences being that *P. radiata* is slightly more delicate in captivity and not quite so easy to wean on to a meat diet.

Common Dragonfish (*top*) and Regal Dragonfish (*bottom*)

Royal-blue Triggerfish
Queen Triggerfish

Triggerfishes (Family Balistidae)

Royal-blue Triggerfish (*Odonus niger*)

This family is characterized by two traits – extreme hardiness and an aggressive nature. Provided that due allowance is made for the latter characteristic, many of the family are suitable for beginners. The Royal-blue or Redfang Triggerfish is in general the least aggressive though individuals may differ greatly in this respect.

The common name triggerfish probably arose because of a curious modification of the dorsal fin into a stiff spike which can be erected at will and then locked or 'triggered' into place. If the fish has swum into a small coral crevice and erected its dorsal and often a similar ventral spike, the collector finds it almost impossible to remove the fish from its lair, so firmly is it wedged into place. The Royal-blue Triggerfish is most common around Ceylon, but does extend in diminishing numbers to the far-eastern coral islands of the Pacific.

The triggerfishes appear to be sensitive to a high concentration of aluminium salts in the water. Respiration is seriously affected and they begin to secrete copious amounts of greyish white mucous. Death usually follows within a few hours unless the fishes are quickly removed to sea water with a normal aluminium concentration.

Feeding triggerfishes seldom presents any major problems. In the wild state, their chosen foods seem to be mostly crustaceans, for example small crabs, prawns, shrimps, lobsters and molluscs. Their massive and powerful jaws are ideally adapted for crushing the latter.

Queen Triggerfish (*Balistes vetula*)

This beautiful species is marred as an aquarium fish by its very belligerent nature, although the keen aquarist may occasionally spot relatively peaceful specimens. The late Professor J. L. B. Smith reported *B. vetula* as being occasionally found off the south-east coast of Africa, but it is only really common in the Caribbean area.

Black Triggerfish (*Melichthys ringens*)

This is one of the few truly circum-tropical species kept in the home sea aquarium. The Black Triggerfish is almost as

Black Triggerfish

Clown Triggerfish

common in the tropical Atlantic as it is in the Indo-Pacific. It is one of the less aggressive triggerfishes and may be kept with most show fishes which are as large as, or preferably larger than, the specimen. A typical community in, for example, an 80 gallon (360 litre) aquarium would be: one *M. ringens,* one large angelfish (*Pomacanthus semicirculatus, P. imperator, P. maculosus* or *P. annularis*), one large *Pterois volitans,* one small 24 in (60 cm) Moray eel and one large wrasse (*Coris angulata* or *Thalassoma lunare*). To establish such a community as peacefully as possible, it would be wise to settle the other species in together for two to three weeks before adding the Black Triggerfish.

Clown Triggerfish (*Balistoides conspicillum*)

When this magnificent creature is exhibited, it is often proclaimed as 'the most expensive fish in the world'. Whereas this may have been true a few years ago, one can now buy a large specimen for almost half the cost of a Majestic Angelfish because of a curious anomaly in the pricing structure of Clown Triggerfishes. The normal rule is 'small fish – low cost, large fish – high cost'. However, this is reversed because the Clown Triggerfish spawns in relatively deep water where the young remain until they attain a length of 6 to 8 in (15 to 20 cm). It is only when they have reached this size that they occasionally wander on to the reef for food, where they can be captured by divers. Hence, small specimens are at a premium and command very high prices.

Variations in triggerfish behaviour reach a peak in this species. Occasional specimens are more ferocious than piranhas. I carry a long scar on my right wrist from a previously mild-mannered 8 in (20 cm) Clown Triggerfish which attacked savagely one day as I rearranged the rockwork in its tank. Most specimens, except in very large tanks, are not to be trusted with any other fishes.

Jigsaw Triggerfish (*Pseudobalistes fuscus*)

This oddly marked fish appears to be limited to the Indian Ocean and the western Indo-Pacific area as it is never listed by any of the Hawaiian, Japanese or Philippino collectors. Most specimens come from the area around Ceylon.

The Jigsaw Triggerfish does not show the extremes of behavioural instability found in the Clown Triggerfish. This is to say that one seldom finds a truly docile Jigsaw Triggerfish, but equally rarely finds a violently aggressive specimen. Provided a sea aquarium of more than 100 gallons (450 litres) is available with plenty of rocky caves and crevices, this species may be kept quite uneventfully with other large show fishes. It would, however, be wise not to include any other triggerfishes in the collection and this applies whatever the size of the aquarium. [This rule also applies to all large show fishes except schooling species such as Yellow Jacks (*Caranx speciosus*) and Striped Catfishes (*Plotosus anguillaris*), etc.]

Yellow-striped Emerald Triggerfish (*Balistapus undulatus*)

This attractively marked but very aggressive triggerfish, sometimes called the Orange-striped or Red-lined Triggerfish, is circum-tropical in distribution except for the tropical Atlantic regions. It is exceptionally tough and disease-free in the sea aquarium but should not be trusted with any except the largest of show fishes in the very large aquarium. The life-span in captivity, like all the triggerfishes, is very long; it is not uncommon for a healthy specimen to live for six to seven years if obtained at a juvenile 2 to 3 in (5 to 7 cm) size. Feeding is quite trouble-free provided that plenty of fresh protein is available.

Picasso Triggerfish (*Rhinecanthus aculeatus*)

The Picasso Triggerfish is so named because of the 'abstract' designs on its flanks. However, it is also known as the 'Humuhumu-nukunuku-a-puaa' Triggerfish in the Hawaiian region. It is often obtainable at 1 to 2 in (2·5 to 5 cm) in length, making it a great favourite because at this size the young fishes are not particularly aggressive.

Filefishes (Family Monocanthidae)

Orange-emerald Filefish (*Oxymonocanthus longirostris*) and Fantailed Filefish (*Pervagor spilosoma*)

According to one of my more reliable overseas collectors, these filefishes reach almost 24 in (60 cm) in length in the wild

Jigsaw Triggerfish

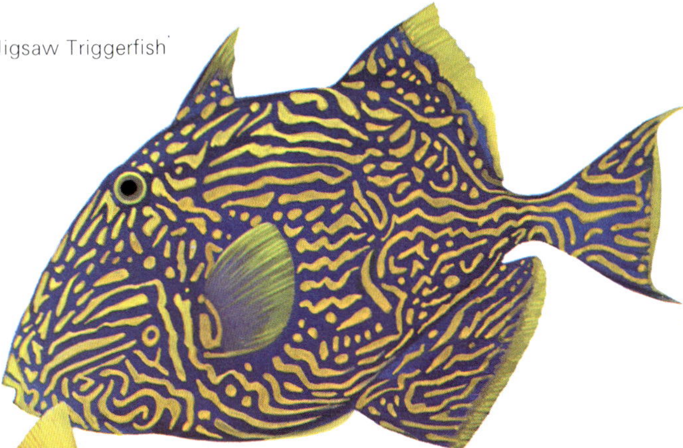

Yellow-striped Emerald Triggerfish

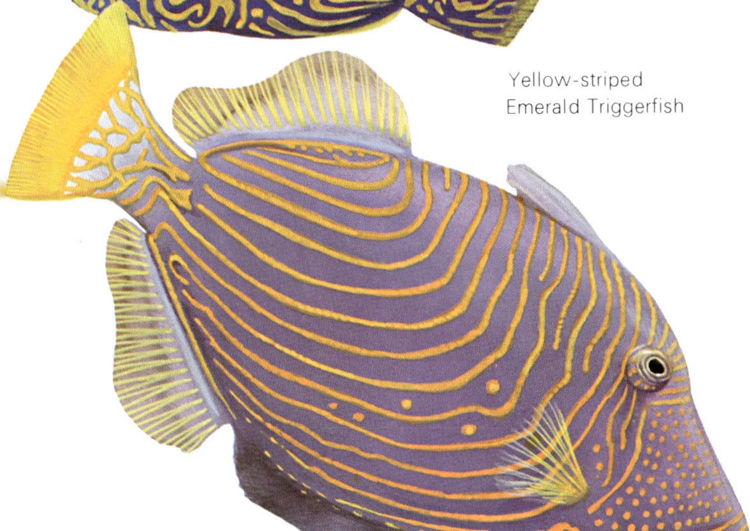

Picasso Triggerfish

state, although they are rarely seen in Europe longer than 2 to 3 in (5 to 7 cm). The Orange-emerald Filefish is also known as the Orange-spotted Filefish and in Australia as the Beaked Leatherjacket.

Filefishes are quite closely related to the triggerfishes and have the same dorsal and ventral spikes for security in their coral retreats, but in behaviour and personality they differ greatly. Filefishes are the very essence of pacifism, even towards members of their own species, and they may be confidently bought by the less experienced marine aquarist, who will have little difficulty in getting them to feed.

Filefishes can, however, be somewhat choosy about foods. On the coral reef they spend the majority of their time pecking at small coral polyps and sponges, and picking tiny crustaceans, molluscs and polyps from rock and dead coral. In the home aquarium, they seem to do best in small groups of two

Orange-emerald Filefish

Fantailed Filefish

or three of their own species and will always begin feeding on newly hatched brine shrimp. After a week or two on this diet, they can be induced to change to vitamin-soaked freeze-dried brine shrimp and later on to prawn eggs and finely chopped squid flesh. From then onwards feeding presents no problem, and within a few days a good specimen will begin eating even a high quality dried flake food such as 'Tetramin'.

Filefishes seem to appreciate, more than triggerfishes, a feed of newly thawed frozen spinach two or three times a week. However, it is as well to remember that this excellent food begins to decompose very quickly once thawed out and may cause severe internal disorders if eaten in a partially rotten state by a hungry fish. Accordingly it must always be kept frozen in the ice box of a domestic refrigerator and a small piece broken off with a hammer ten minutes before feeding time. This can then be thawed and immediately fed to the fishes.

Tetrasoma gibbosus

Boxfishes or trunkfishes (Family Ostraciontidae)
Tetrasoma gibbosus

This fish is a great favourite with the ladies, possibly owing to its whimsical appearance and appealing eyes. It has sometimes been called the 'Hovercraft' because its nearly transparent, rapidly beating pectoral fins cause it to move through the water with no visible means of propulsion. Furthermore, in general shape, with the high domed back and almost flat ventral surface, it is not unlike a hovercraft.

These fishes are found throughout the Indo-Pacific area but are never common and always command a good price when available. A good sized adult specimen will reach almost 10 in (25 cm) in length, when its general proportions resemble those of a small football with the bottom removed. However, most specimens suitable for the home sea aquarium are tennis ball size or smaller and make most endearing pets, quickly becoming tame and learning to recognize their owner. I had one specimen so tame that it would swim on to a hand, submerged palm uppermost just under the surface, and allow itself to be lifted completely out of the water for a few seconds. This behaviour shows the extraordinary trust coral fishes can develop – to a degree not paralleled among freshwater fishes. For any fishes other than mudskippers, lungfishes, eels and a few others, such an action represents completely abnormal behaviour requiring enormous faith and adaptability. No difficulty is experienced in feeding this species, all foods being eagerly accepted.

Cowfish (*Lactoria cornutus*)

These 'armour-plated' boxfishes are completely circum-tropical and are excellent community fishes. They are easy to feed and strongly resistant to most diseases.

Ostracion lentiginosum

These boxfishes, although beautifully marked, should be treated with great caution when introduced into an already established aquarium. If the water is not clean or if they are attacked and scared by the existing members of the tank, they react by producing a highly toxic frothy substance around the mouth. This foam not only proves fatal for the offending attacker but also for all the other fishes in the aquarium including *Ostracion lentiginosum*.

Cowfish

Ostracion lentiginosum

Porcupine fishes (Family Diodontidae)

Common Porcupine fish (*Diodon hystrix*)

There are many fishes similar in appearance in the genus *Diodon,* and most are offered for sale from time to time indiscriminately labelled as '*Diodon hystrix*'. However, there is very little variation among the species with regard to their needs and behaviour.

The Porcupine fish, like the pufferfishes, is distinguished by its ability to swallow huge amounts of water, inflating itself to many times its original size. Inflated it looks like a football with the face of a pekinese dog and the tail of a fish. Occasionally, when badly panicked, the Porcupine fish makes the mistake of coming to the surface and inflating itself with air. Whereas most specimens can release this air when the source of provocation is removed, a few seem to have a defective release mechanism, and consequently float around on the surface, dehydrating until they perish.

When in the inflated state the spines covering the body stand out at an angle. It is believed that by inflating itself the large spiky fish looks less attractive to a predator. It will be apparent to most people, therefore, that since this self-inflating ability is only used as a response to fright, it is extremely cruel to continually terrify a captive Porcupine fish in order to demonstrate the phenomenon.

Common Porcupine fish

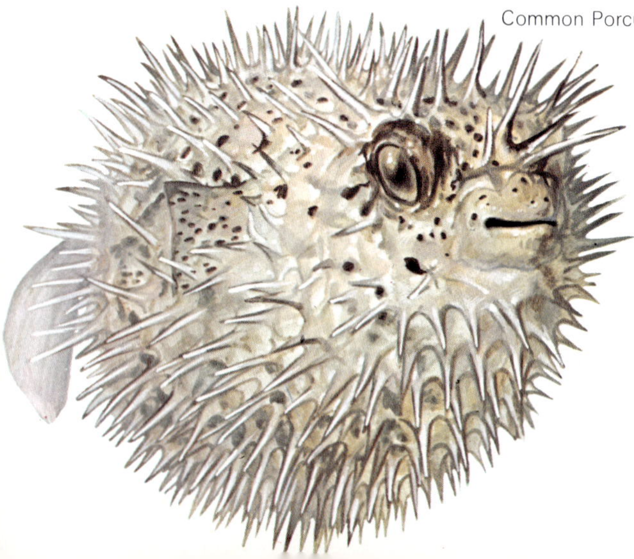

The porcupine fishes are easy to feed on any kind of proteinaceous matter such as earthworm, squid, mussel, steak, heart and washed, chopped liver.

Pufferfishes (Family Canthigasteridae)

Diamond-flecked Pufferfish (*Canthigaster margaritatus*)

This animal is very common throughout the Central and Indo-Pacific. It is hardy and resistant to disease and consequently easily shipped – a combination of circumstances producing a fish that is always readily available at low prices. This species will eat any kind of flesh, once acclimatized to aquarium life.

Minstrel Pufferfish (*Canthigaster valentini*)

The comments for the previous species apply to the Minstrel Pufferfish although it is rather more rare in the wild. In common with the Diamond-flecked Pufferfish, it is able to make an angry grunting noise when upset.

Diamond-flecked Pufferfish

Minstrel Pufferfish

Discosoma anemone

Fanworm

Live coral head of *Goniopora*

INVERTEBRATES FOR THE AQUARIUM

Coelenterates

These animals are characterized by a hollow tubular body, usually closed at one end (the foot) with an opening at the other (the mouth), fringed with tentacles. Two groups suitable for the home sea aquarium are anemones and corals.

Anemones

Generally the hardiest anemones are the genus *Discosoma.* These animals vary in size from a mouth disc as little as 2 in (5 cm) to specimens several feet in diameter. To keep the larger anemones a large tank, of minimum size 72 × 24 × 18 in (180 × 60 × 45 cm), is required.

Anemones are very susceptible to sudden changes in water quality and, when introducing one to the aquarium, at least an hour should be taken in slowly mixing the waters together. Their vitamin requirements, particularly of B_{12} and B_1, appear to be quite high, and a good vitamin concentrate should be added to the small pieces of meat they are fed every other day or so. When buying an anemone check that all the tentacles and the oral disc are fully extended and look healthy. If any part is collapsed or appears to be breaking up, the specimen should be rejected.

Anemones of the genus *Stoichactis* have an oral disc covered in thousands of minute, densely packed tentacles, giving an impression of coarse velvet. They are not as tough as the *Discosoma* species and are really for the advanced marine aquarist.

Living corals

These tiny colonial animals, individually called polyps, are essentially for the purely natural system aquarium as they are one of the few natural methods of mechanical filtration. The polyp has the same coelenterate body plan but on a much smaller scale than the anemone, and it extracts calcium and magnesium salts from the water thus building up a hard limey tube around itself. Corals and the larger tube or fan worms are filter feeders, continually removing planktonic organisms from the water.

Echinoderms

All the echinoderms (spiny-skinned animals) exhibit a common body design, i.e., they are radially symmetrical. This means there is no bi-lateral symmetry (no right- and left-hand side) as in higher animals such as mammals, birds, etc., but that there is symmetry in form in a plane at right angles to the central axis. The echinoderms commonly seen in the marine aquarium are the starfishes, sea urchins and sea-cucumbers.

Starfishes

Almost all the starfishes kept in tropical marine aquaria appear to be browsers, i.e. they rasp small organisms from living rocks, etc. Consequently they should be kept only in semi-natural or natural marine tanks as they would slowly starve to death in a clinical system aquarium.

Sea-urchins

These invertebrates and particularly the Black Sea-urchins do very well in the marine aquarium on a diet of prawn, steak and earthworm. They appear to be omnivorous in the wild and in the aquarium relish a piece of lettuce or spinach twice a week. All foods for the sea-urchin should be dropped into the spines, which will then slowly manoeuvre the food down and round to the mouth (Aristotle's lantern), located in the centre of the ventral surface of the animal.

Molluscs

The marine molluscs which are best for the sea aquarium are, in order of hardiness, cowries, conches, clams, nudibranchs and flame scallops. The cowries, in which the mantle from time to time flows completely around the shell hiding it from view, are very hardy in old established semi-natural or natural system aquaria. Most species will graze continually on the algae which coat all surfaces within the aquarium, although they should be occasionally offered small pieces of finely chopped meat. These comments also apply to the conches, which move around the tank with a cumbersome, but amusing, hopping motion. The beautiful shell-less nudibranchs graze on sessile planktonic organisms, whilst both the clams and flame scallops are filter feeders.

Red Starfish

Long-spined Sea-urchin

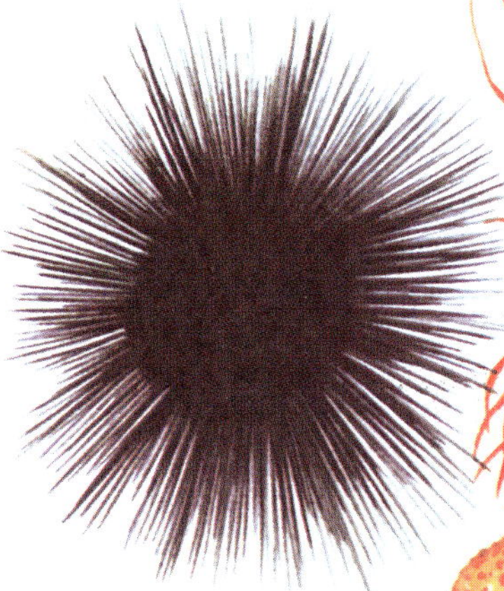

Nudibranch mollusc

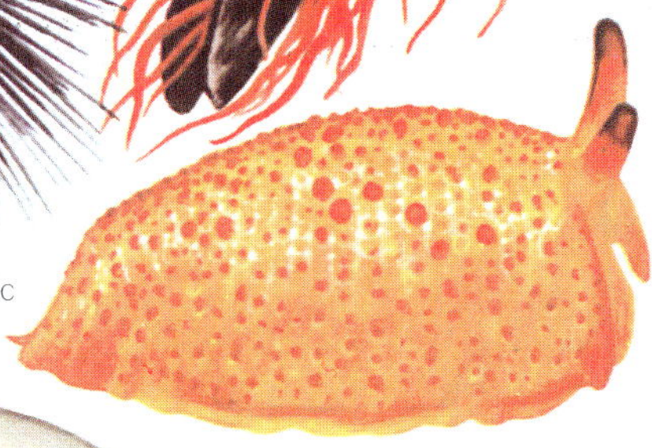

Cowrie

Octopus (*Octopus*)

The octopus is a member of the molluscan class Cephalopoda, which also includes the cuttlefishes and squids. In these highly developed invertebrates there is a tendency for the shell to become vestigial, with a corresponding increase in activity, manoeuvrability and ferocity. An amazingly complex nervous and sensory system has developed and predatory habits which usually go with them. The eye has developed to such an extent that it rivals even that of the mammals in efficiency. The foot of the octopus has developed into a circle of arms around the mouth well equipped with a pair of horny parrot-like jaws capable of giving a nasty bite.

A small specimen between 18 and 30 in (45 and 75 cm) in length can make a fascinating subject for study. Feeding is quite easy to achieve provided that the animal's territorial requirement is catered for. The aquarium should be as large as possible and contain many nooks and crannies, crevices, caves and shelves. With an animal as nervous and psychologically complicated as the octopus, detailed attention to the design of the aquarium decor is as vital as attention to the water quality.

Having created a suitably complicated and reassuringly natural habitat for the octopus, the tank should be filled with the best quality synthetic sea water available. Several days should be allowed under full filtration and aeration for the water to mature. For gravel to cover the undergravel filter use old 'ripe' gravel which has been lightly washed in clean, warm sea water. (Never wash matured gravel with fresh water for this will destroy the nitrifying bacteria coating every particle. Never throw matured sea aquarium gravel away – it is precious.)

The octopus should be introduced into the aquarium very slowly, taking perhaps thirty-five to forty-five minutes, and in almost total darkness. When the waters have been gradually mixed, the octopus, if it has not already done so, may be encouraged to climb out of the polythene bag into its new home. Feeding should be attempted the following day with small pieces of prawn, shrimp or crab flesh. Although most species of octopus are nocturnal feeders, they are such gluttonous animals that they can be easily encouraged to feed and disport themselves during daylight hours.

It is almost impossible to keep fishes with an octopus since they are nearly always caught and eaten by the octopus within a few days. However, a well-fed octopus will not usually interfere with live corals, tubeworms, starfishes, sea-urchins or anemones.

Octopus

Crustaceans

The crustaceans include the crabs, prawns, shrimps, lobsters and crayfishes. Many are exceptionally hardy and ideal for the beginner's marine invertebrate aquarium.

Boxing Shrimp (*Stenopus hispidus*)

This spectacular little crustacean does very well in the sea aquarium provided that it is regularly fed. Many people buy these animals as scavengers and then, because they have a new aquarium with 'unripened' gravel (lacking a population of nitrifying bacteria), embark on a programme of sparse feeding, forgetting all about *Stenopus*, waiting on the bottom of the tank for food which never falls down to it. The answer to this problem is either to feed the animals individually with tiny pieces of meat impaled on the end of a plastic knitting needle, or to withhold the purchase of Boxing Shrimps until such time as the gravel has completely matured bacterially (up to three months).

The ferocity of Boxing Shrimps to each other (except during the mating period) is startling. In view of this intra-specific aggression which invariably ends in the death of one if not both of the combatants, it is extremely cruel to house more than one shrimp in a tank smaller than 150 gallons (675 litres).

Mantis shrimps

These animals are responsible for those tiny pyramids of sand often seen on the sea bed in the tropics. In the aquarium they rarely prove to be a hardy animal and only very advanced marine aquarists should consider attempts at culturing the species.

Hermit crabs

These are crustaceans in which the normal protective chitinous exoskeleton is absent on the abdomen. To protect its vulnerable parts from predators, the hermit crab adopts an empty shell of a univalve mollusc (for example a whelk) in to which it can safely tuck its abdomen. When the animal grows too large for the shell, it discards it and adopts a new, larger one. In the sea aquarium hermit crabs are very interesting and hardy scavengers.

Hermit Crab
Boxing Shrimp
Fairy Shrimp
Crayfish
Mantis Shrimp

Marine live food

Examples: shrimps, prawns, sandhoppers, crab and lobster flesh and the liver, mantle and foot of freshly killed mussels

ADVANTAGES	DISADVANTAGES
May well provide vital trace elements. Usually stays alive in the tank if not eaten immediately.	Unless properly quarantined, marine live food may well transmit diseases to aquarium fishes. It is difficult to keep alive in store.

FEEDING AQUARIUM ANIMALS

This topic and water management are probably the two most difficult aspects of sea aquarium keeping for the beginner to master. Whereas there are certain clearly laid down steps detailing the methods of establishing a marine tank for either the natural, semi-natural or clinical systems, so much of what separates a good 'feeder' and good 'manager' from their less fortunate alternatives, is attributable to experience, common sense and that most intangible quality 'salty-fingers'.

The general rule that should always be adhered to is 'a little food often'. This principle is most vitally important during the first critical three months, during which time the *nitrifying potential* of the aquarium (the ability of the bacteria in the gravel to oxidize waste matter to harmless nitrates) is steadily increasing but not at a high enough level to tolerate careless over feeding. Throughout the whole of this period, unless de-ionizing resins are being used in a power filter, the water will have a low and constantly diminishing nitrite reading. This is one of the many reasons why the beginner is urged to keep damselfishes for the first three months or, if he

Other live food

Examples: earthworms, whiteworms, grindal worms, *Daphia, Tubifex,* mosquito larvae, young livebearers (mollies, guppies, platies, swordtails)

ADVANTAGES	DISADVANTAGES
Cannot carry diseases to aquarium fishes and is fairly easy to keep alive in store. This live food can be readily obtained.	Some fishes will not take to these foods initially and will require patient weaning before they will feed readily.

Comparison of the advantages and disadvantages of marine and other live aquarium food.

prefers larger fishes, snapperfishes, triggerfishes, dragonfishes or *Platax orbicularis.*

It is a good idea to get into the habit of determining when an animal is in a feeding mood. Good general pointers to be watched for are an alertness of eye and movement, which in the case of butterfly fishes and angelfishes, shows itself as a series of active, close-range examinations of pieces of coral and rockwork, with the occasional pecking at real or imagined objects thereon. The more active or predatory animals such as snapperfishes, triggerfishes, dragonfishes, wrasses and sharks will often show their hunger by chasing up and down the aquarium in a generally alert fashion.

The next precautions to take are that the correct type of food is offered to the fishes in correct particle size. For example, it would be ridiculous to offer spinach to a dragonfish and as foolish to offer a single prawn egg to a 9 in (23 cm) Emperor Snapper, or a half-inch cube of prawn flesh to a butterfly fish.

DISEASES OF FISHES

Oodinium

The most important and only really common disease of tropical marine fishes is caused by the protozoan dinoflagellate *Oodinium ocellatum*. It is particularly virulent in its attacks upon juvenile fishes – especially in an overcrowded aquarium. It is a swift killer unless promptly treated with one of several available brands of medication (e.g. 'Cuprazin'). The parasite cannot normally be seen on the body until the disease is advanced, and often incurable. Even then the greyish-white to fawn-yellow cysts are so small that they are unlikely to be seen unless the fish is viewed head on with rear lighting. Primarily the parasites attack the gill filaments and it is not until they have weakened the fish by partial asphyxiation that they can establish themselves on the body. The best indication of an incipient *Oodinium* infection is a sudden increase in the respiratory rate (shown by the number of movements made by the gill covers). A normal rate for a healthy fish is 80 to 110 gill movements per minute. It must be remembered that factors other than *Oodinium* infection can affect the respiratory rate, but if the *p*H, specific gravity, temperature, nitrite and ammonia levels are all within normal limits and yet the breathing rate is increased, it is safe to assume that the fishes are suffering from an *Oodinium* infection.

Possibly *Oodinium* disease is latent in all marine fishes and only develops under physical, chemical or psychological stress. Aquarists are strongly advised to treat all new fishes with a good *Oodinium* cure as soon as they are settled into their aquarium.

Lymphocystis

This disease is most common among Caribbean fishes kept in water which has previously contained Indo-Pacific fishes. However, any marine fishes can be infected by *Lymphocystis* and, because it is a viral infection, no known medication is effective against it, not even antibiotics. However, one need not destroy fishes suffering from *Lymphocystis* as is sometimes recommended. Provided that the cysts are cleanly cut away and the cut areas are sterilized by a light brushing of Myxazin disinfectant solution an otherwise healthy fish will make a rapid recovery. Alternatively treat with Paragon.

Fishes suffering from *Oodinium* disease (*left*) and *Lymphocystis*

White spot disease

This is caused by a parasite in the genus *Cryptocaryon* which embeds itself in the skin and produces greyish-white hemispherical cysts about one quarter the size of a pin head. It is less dangerous but more difficult to cure than *Oodinium* and is treated in the same way.

Benedenia

Large, grey-white, triangular flukes fix on to the body with the apex towards the tail. Large angelfishes subjected to a high nitrite level often succumb to this disease. It is easily cured by treating with Sterazin and is one of the easiest diseases to detect.

Ichthyophonus fungus

This attacks the internal organs and there is as yet no practical cure. It is extremely rare among coral fishes. Infection usually takes the form of the fish developing a ravenous appetite but losing weight rapidly. I have had limited success in prolonging the life of the fishes with daily injections of streptomycin, penicillin and vitamin B_{12} for five days. This is a widely distributed species of fungus.

Saprolegnia – type fungal infections

These appear to be extremely rare in captive coral fishes. Should they occur they can be cleared up in a matter of days with 'cuprazin' or 'sterazin'; if invertebrates are present treatment must take place in a separate tank.

Finrot and bodyrot

These loose terms cover the effect of several types of pathogenic bacteria on coral fishes. If the quality of the water is good and the animals are not deficient in any vitamins, such attacks are very rare. If the water is occasionally ozonized, they are virtually non-existent. As ozonizers are still expensive, it should be stated that an effective cure is to apply a bactericidal solution such as 'Myxazin', proflavine, mercurochrome or a solution of one teaspoonful of 16 vols hydrogen peroxide solution in an eggcupful of water. Avoid contact of the hydrogen peroxide with eyes or gills.

White spot

Benedenia

Finrot and bodyrot

GENERAL HINTS FOR THE BEGINNER

Never overfeed your fishes. Keep your tank as clean as possible by removing any uneaten food. Introduce as much variety as possible into the diet.

Never overcrowd the aquarium. It is better to have a few fishes in radiant health than many gulping fishes, battle-scarred through fighting over inadequate territory.

Never open a travelling box containing marine fishes in strong light, and always make the transition from polythene bag to aquarium as gradually as possible.

Never add small fishes to an aquarium which already contains large and well-established fishes, unless of course you have expert knowledge of the natures of both the resident fishes and the new addition.

Never remove invertebrate animals from the water when transferring them from aquarium to aquarium. They should be placed in a water-filled polythene bag held underwater and

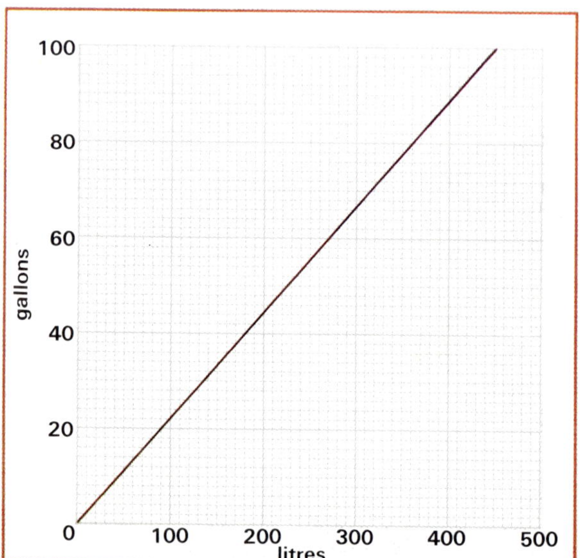

released in the same fashion. This will prevent pockets of air being trapped in their bodies which they may not be able to get rid of.

Never use lead to weight down a floating object. Lead (and the traces of zinc which it often contains), copper, brass, bronze and aluminium are all toxic in excess to marine life. It is safer to use a piece of silicone rubber, P.V.C., A.B.S. or some other non-toxic plastic to weight a piece of coral or rock.

Always check regularly the specific gravity, temperature and *p*H of your water.

Always be aware of the following early indications of fouling in sea water: frothing at the water surface; water becoming cloudy; fishes breathing more rapidly than normal (could also be disease); water producing fetid odour.

Always provide as much coral and rockwork as possible for shy species.

Always check all fishes are present at feeding time.

Always ensure that all corals, shells, gorgonian and sea fan skeletons are thoroughly cured (and that no trace of chlorine odour clings to them) before using them inside the sea aquarium.

Aquarium volume (*left*) and temperature (*below*) conversion graphs.

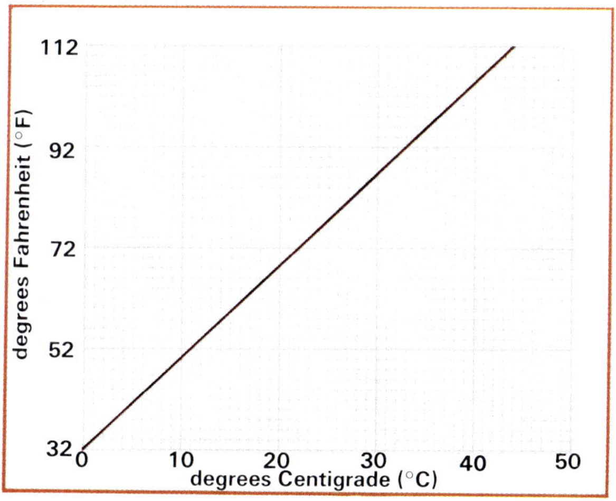

PLACES TO VISIT

In Britain
Belle Vue Zoo Aquarium, Manchester
Brighton Aquarium and Dolphinarium
London Zoo Aquarium
Plymouth Marine Aquarium
Poole Aquarium
Birdworld and Aquarium, Farnham, Surrey

In USA
Cleveland Aquarium, Cleveland, Ohio
John G. Shedd Aquarium, Chicago, Illinois
Aquarium of Niagara Falls, Niagara Falls, New York
Steinhart Aquarium, San Francisco, California

INDEX

Page numbers in **bold** type refer to illustrations.